KATHY BROWN'S RECIPES
for
EASY CONTAINER GARDENING

KATHY BROWN'S RECIPES
for
EASY CONTAINER GARDENING

MICHAEL JOSEPH
LONDON

MICHAEL JOSEPH LTD
Published by the Penguin Group
27 Wrights Lane, London W8 5TZ
Viking Penguin Inc., 375 Hudson Street, New York,
New York 10014, USA
Penguin Books Australia Ltd, Ringwood, Victoria, Australia
Penguin Books Canada Ltd,
10 Alcorn Avenue, Toronto, Ontario, Canada M4V 3B2
Penguin Books (NZ) Ltd,
182–190 Wairau Road, Auckland 10, New Zealand

Penguin Books Ltd,
Registered Offices: Harmondsworth, Middlesex, England

First published in Great Britain 1995

Some of the recipes appearing in this book
were originally published in
Creative Container Gardening copyright © Kathleen Brown 1987
Seasonal Container Gardening copyright © Kathleen Brown 1991
This volume copyright © Kathy Brown 1995

Printed in Belgium by Proost

ISBN 0 7181 3860 0

The moral right of the author has been asserted

Note about the photographs
All the photographs are by
Timothy Woodcock apart from
those appearing in the following
recipes which are by Dan
Whiting of Colegrave Seeds:
2 3 6 7 15 16 17 20 25 26 27
28 29 30 31 32 33 44 45 61

AUTUMN, WINTER AND SPRING WINDOW BOXES AND HANGING BASKETS

AUTUMN, WINTER AND SPRING WICKER BASKETS

AUTUMN, WINTER AND SPRING URNS AND POTS

INTRODUCTION

I have chosen recipes from *Creative Container Gardening* and *Seasonal Container Gardening* which together represent a series of simple planting schemes. Added to these are twenty new recipes which include many of today's best bedding plants.

The planting schemes are written in my unique 'recipe' style, captured in their own superb photograph. Each has details on the size of the container, site, when to plant it up and when it will look its best; every one has a full list of plant ingredients, step-by-step method, and details on aftercare. Just like a cookery book, the idea is both inspirational and practical. Here the use of the recipe formula takes the mystique out of gardening; these planting schemes are all achievable.

CONTAINERS

Each container is given its own detailed dimensions and description. This allows you to either seek exactly the same one, or adjust the planting scheme to suit your own pot or trough if the size is different.

I am indebted to certain companies for lending me containers so that I could extend the range of the ones planted up for the new recipes. The hanging baskets came from Erin Marketing Ltd. You will find both 30cm (12") and 35cm (14") diameter baskets in these recipes. I prefer the latter which allows larger planting schemes and more root run, but the smaller basket is good where you want a more compact, neater shape and obviously the plants will cost less.

The stone pots and vase came from Kingfisher Ornamental Stone. They came in two colours, grey Portland, and warmer Cotswold. The Terra Perma range came from Richard Sankey and Son Ltd. They are a relatively new product in the UK, made of light-weight polymers to look like terracotta but are much cheaper, frost proof, and won't break if dropped. They are also extremely light to move around. They are a bonus to the elderly or those with back problems, and ideal for roof gardens.

The window boxes, Swap Tub and barrel came from Trevis Garden Products. The window box and Swap Tub have plastic liners which helps preserve the wood and, at the same time, makes them easier to plant up, move around or bring on in the greenhouse. Duplicate liners are also available. In the past, Whichford Potteries and Olive Tree Trading have both lent terracotta pots, Renaissance Casting Ltd has lent lead containers and Haddonstone Ltd has allowed the use of their stone pots. All these are represented in the recipes included from my previous books.

PLANTING TIME
First, mid spring/early summer before the main summer bedding can be safely planted out. This is a period of rapid growth when pansies, primroses, polyanthus, bellis daisies, violas, herbs, Cinderella stocks, cinerarias and ranunculus can all be used to create a riot of colour.

Second, mid May to mid June depending on your location and which plants are being used. This is traditionally recognised as being the main planting season for containers. Busy Lizzies, geraniums, lobelia, gazanias, marigolds etc are all available. The choice of bedding plants is at its greatest.

Third, the late summer/early autumn period. At this stage, most summer plantings are past their best, and yet we may have several weeks of mild weather. This is a time to use ornamental kale and cabbages, winter-flowering pansies, violas, ivies and hebes. For those in sheltered urban areas try colourful pot-grown cyclamen and solanum. True, they are tender and you will loose them sometimes before Christmas; however, if you plant in early September, they should give you several weeks of superb colour. When frost threatens, cover them with newspaper or move the pot inside.

Fourth, the longest period of all taking the pots from autumn right through to spring. This is a time of two-tier planting using winter bedding plants underplanted with bulbs. Winter-flowering pansies, polyanthus and wallflowers look wonderful with daffodils and tulips flowering above them. There are so many ideas to choose from.

PLANTS
Some of the plants in the new recipes deserve special mention. Outstanding among them is *Lobelia erinus* 'Riviera Blue Splash'. Its violet-blue throat and edge contrasts perfectly with its white centre. It is used in Recipe 17 with very strong pinks. It is also planted in Recipe 30 where it combines beautifully with other 'violet blue' shades of petunias, ageratum, and trailing convolvulus; together they look sumptuous with the creamy new marigold called

Tagetes 'Vanilla'. Another newcomer is the pink and white *Nicotiana* 'Havana Appleblossom' which makes a perfect match for *Petunia* 'Express Light Salmon'. This is a dreamy creation which looks especially lovely by evening sunlight; see Recipe 29.

In vibrant contrast are the amazing *Petunia surfinia*. These trailing Japanese petunias have become extremely popular in recent years and produce a cascade of dazzling purple, mauve, pink and white. Recipe 20 combines them with mauvy-blue scaevolas, another trailing plant which grows in a complementary fashion but branches upwards. *Dianthus* 'Strawberry Parfait' is strongly recommended for any eyecatching display in the height of summer. It creates a mound of colour, deep red in the centre, softening a little to crushed strawberry, with white around the edge; see Recipe 27.

Autumn and spring plantings bring the new daisy *Bellis perennis* 'Robella', with its large pink flowers, which combine wonderfully with blue primroses and polyanthus; see Recipe 61. For a mid to late spring planting, try 'Cinderella' stocks. They have an excellent scent and a good range of colours which blend superbly with 'Turbo' pansies; see Recipe 2. Ranunculus offer a more strident colour display for sheltered containers.

Clematis are included as an important plant to establish up a trellis or patio wall. I chose Pennell's charming blue 'H F Young' for Recipe 7, but there are a host of other large flowered hybrids to plant in a whole range of mauves, white, lilac and pink. *Clematis montana* or *C. alpina* would be suitable for a spring display.

I have tried to use plants which are widely available, many of them based on the Colegrave Seed Catalogue which is used by many of our leading bedding plant growers. However, I recognise that every garden centre stocks different varieties and trying to find exact plant names can be very frustrating. Don't be put off. While all my recipes have been tried and tested with those plants listed in the ingredients, they will also work if plants are substituted. Changing one lobelia or geranium for another won't matter at all, although the colour scheme will obviously be slightly different. Anyway, you may prefer alternative colours. I love to use salmon pinks, reds, oranges, and violet-blues. Others might feel more at home with mauves and purples. Some will like plain coloured busy lizzies and petunias, others will

10

like the stars and frills. One of the joys of container gardening is that we have such a wide range of colours and effects from which to choose. Experimenting can be such fun!

Bulbs: All the bulbs mentioned are the popular varieties and will be available at any of the hundreds of garden centres supplied by O.A. Taylor and Sons Ltd of Holbeach. They will also be found at many others. Some of the dwarf varieties are extremely popular and supplies can run low; therefore, buy them as early as you can. You don't have to plant them immediately, just keep them in a cool dry place until you are ready.

BUDGET PLANTING

This book includes a mixture of recipes to suit all pockets. Many of the plants can be grown from seed. Some of them such as tagetes, *Begonia semperflorens*, lobelia, salvias, nicotiana, petunia, verbena, parsley, and busy lizzies can be bought in polystyrene strips, or packs of four or sometimes six at a time. This usually makes the individual plants much cheaper, and although the plants may be smaller than those growing in their own pots, they will soon grow into fine specimens. Moreover, small plants are far easier to cope with when side-planting hanging baskets. Money can also be saved by recycling plants. Remove spring flowering perennials and ivies in May and June from their winter and spring containers. Plant them out in the garden where they can grow on ready to be lifted and divided in the autumn and so used again for the next season's containers. Likewise, fuchsias, geraniums, tuberous begonias and many other plants can be overwintered and so use again the following year, *see* page 14.

COMPOST

Always use fresh compost in your containers. It will be expensive in time and effort but the rewards will certainly justify the cost. Not only is it sterilised and therefore weed free, but its composition is ideal for rapid growth. There are several brands available but Levington Hanging Basket and Container Compost is particularly good with its especially designed re-wetting agent which enables the soil to take up water quickly and effectively. This is invaluable for all spring and summer containers where drying out is one of the major problems. It is also suitable for winter containers as it drains freely and will not waterlog. If required Levington have a peat-free compost made from re-cycled natural materials. This also has the re-wetting agent incorporated but due to the nature of the compost may need watering more often than the peat-based equivalent.

The heavier soil-based mixes using the John Innes formula are excellent where the planting scheme is of a long-term nature. For example, John Innes No 3 is advised for the clematis barrel in Recipe 7. Not only does it contain slow-release fertilisers in its mix, but its extra drainage helps to keep an open texture and allows good long-term growth. Its loam content makes it much heavier so it is useful for windier locations where pots might be liable to blow over.

The amount of compost required will depend on the inside measurements of the container. As a rough guide for an *oblong* container such as a trough or window box, take the length, width and depth in centimetres and multiply to arrive at the volume required. For example, a deep trough 87.5cm long, 20cm deep and 12.5cm wide would need $87.5 \times 20 \times 12.5 = 21,875$ cu cm = 21.9 litres (1000 cu cm = 1 litre)

If you have *round* barrel or pot, measure the radius (ie half the diameter) and the depth. The formula is $3.14 \times$ radius squared $\times$ depth. For example, a large wooden half-barrel with a diameter of 60cm (= radius 30cm) and depth of 37.5cm, would need: 3.14 × 30 × 30 × 37.5 = 105,975 cu cm = 106 litres.

In both cases these are generous estimates as the space taken up by the 5–7.5cm (2–3") of drainage material usually recommended, and the 2.5cm (1") gap between the compost and the top of the container, are included in the above calculation. However, these adjustments have been allowed for in the recipe calculations.

DRAINAGE
It is vital that every container has adequate drainage holes. New Terra Perma or plastic containers may need holes knocking through. Winter containers, in particular, suffer from waterlogging so take particular care. Broken pieces of polystyrene make ideal drainage material, they are light, free and do not deteriorate. Broken crocks are also recommended. Either one will ensure that the compost and roots are kept away from the drainage holes, so that the latter remain free from blockage.

WATERING
Check that the compost is moist with the finger test. Touch it to feel whether it is dry or not. If the compost sticks, it is damp. If your finger comes away clean, it is dry. Summer containers and, in particular, summer hanging baskets dry out very quickly. The addition of water-storing granules such as Erin's Waterwell will help a great deal. Mix them in with the compost when you first plant up in May and they will work throughout the summer. They don't mean that watering becomes unnecessary, but they do reduce watering times significantly in very hot weather. It is better to water at soil level rather than from overhead as some flowers are delicate and spoil badly, especially petunias, while other plants such as begonias have large leaves and water just runs off them onto the ground. Water in the early morning or evening if possible, but avoid splashing the foliage when the sun is out or ugly burn marks will appear.

Autumn, winter and, particularly, spring containers need water, especially if they are close to the house but *never* water in frosty weather. Better, then, to keep the compost on the dry side. Extra drainage material will help in these conditions.

FEEDING
New composts provide a store of nutrients for the first four

to six weeks, but after that the plants will be on a strict diet. Results will depend very much on the amount of extra food given. Long-term food sachets or granules are available for use at the time of planting, as a one-off feed, or liquid applications can be made throughout the flowering season. There are many excellent brands on the market, especially Miracle-Gro. In order to obtain the maximum benefit, water first, then apply the feed.

DEADHEADING
Deadheading means the removal of faded flower heads, together with the seed capsule which is busy forming at the base of the petals. Once plants have gone to seed, they are less keen to produce flowers; therefore, the deadheading process is vital in prolonging the flowering period. Do it every few days and you will be well rewarded.

PEST CONTROL
Slugs and snails do terrible damage to plants, especially when conditions are damp and plants are wet after rain or the evening watering session. Keep a constant watch. Choose a method which is as friendly as possible to other garden life. Greenfly, whitefly and blackfly are the other main problem. Keep your plants well fed and watered so they will be far more healthy and less likely to be attacked. But if you do see a problem starting, then use one of the 'safe' brands available. Act quickly. Aphids have no notion of birth control and infestations soon build up!

BEGINNING AND END OF SEASON CARE
Begonias (tuberous): SPRING Start tubers into growth in March by placing them on top of moist compost, hollow side uppermost, so that they nestle into it without being entirely covered. Put them in a warm place (such as an airing cupboard) until the tubers show signs of new growth. Keep them moist, and when the first leaves appear bring them into the light. No artificial heat is now needed, but they should remain in a frost-free place, and then gradually hardened off before being planted out towards end May or early June.

AUTUMN Their leaves will start to turn yellow which indicates the start of the drying-off process. Lift before any frost damage, label and plant temporarily in moist peat. Gradually reduce their supply of water and when the foliage has died off completely, remove the tubers, clean off the compost, and store in a cool, frost-free environment 7–10C (45–50F) covered with dry peat. Give the occasional light watering to prevent the tubers from shrivelling.

Fuchsias SPRING Prune back the old wood to within two or three nodes of last season's growth. When the first leaves appear, it is time to start watering again. Harden off the plants gradually in mid-May, ready to be planted out end May or early June.

AUTUMN Pot the plants into 15–22.5cm (6–9") pots, label them, and keep in a frost-free greenhouse, shed or loft over the winter. Gradually reduce their water supply until the leaves drop off. The plants need hardly any water until the spring.

Geraniums (Pelargoniums) SPRING When new growth begins, gradually increase the water supply. Harden off the plants gradually in mid-May ready to be planted out end May or early June.

AUTUMN Remove plants from summer containers, cut back top growth to 10–15cm (4–6"), removing all leaves, and trim the roots. Label, and plant individually in compost in a 10cm (4") pot. Keep them frost-free, in a greenhouse or on a windowsill inside the house. Water them well to begin with and then keep only barely moist.

Campanula isophylla, Chlorophytum comosum (spider plant), *Chrysanthemum (Argyranthemum) frutescens* (white marguerite), *Convolvulus mauritanicus, Gazanias, Helichrysum, Glechoma hederacea* (Nepeta) *Plectranthus, Sedum sieboldii* and *Tradescantia* SPRING As new growth appears, gradually increase the watering. Harden off gradually before planting out end May to early June.

AUTUMN Pot up and place in a greenhouse or on a light, cool windowsill away from any danger of frost. Water occasionally.

ACKNOWLEDGEMENTS

I would like to thank Mike Dixon for making the National Patio Festival possible, thereby enabling me to have the support of Colegrave Seeds; Erin, Kingfisher, Sankey Terra Perma, and Trevis containers; Fison's Horticulture; Miracle-Gro, and Pennell's Nurseries as well as the other National Patio Festival partners. Very special thanks go to John Whitehead and Alan Miles for all their help and advice.

LATE SPRING AND EARLY SUMMER CONTAINERS

1   INSTANT SPRING AND EARLY SUMMER COLOUR

Sometimes you feel you just can't wait until the end of May to plant out your pots for the summer. Here is an example of what you can put together to achieve lovely colour from early April onwards even though night frosts may still occur.

Site
Any aspect.

Container
Small terracotta pot: 25 cm (10") in diameter, 20cm (8") deep.

Planting Time
Early April onwards.

Looks its Best
From time of planting to June.

Ingredients
    3 pansies *Viola* 'Turbo Azure Blue'
    1 strip of pink daisies *Bellis perennis* 'Tasso Rose'
    7 litres of compost
    Drainage material such as small pieces of polystyrene

Method
1 Cover the base of the container with 2.5cm (1") drainage material and add 7.5cm (3") compost.
2 Plant the pansies towards the centre of the pot and fill the gaps with compost.
3 Carefully separate the bellis plants and plant them around the edge.
4 Water well. Add more compost if necessary.

Aftercare
Water generously, particularly in warm spells. Pansies

especially like a lot of moisture. Feed with a proprietary brand as directed, at least every two weeks. Both pansies and daisies will flower longer if deadheaded. Discard them when they have finally given up flowering.

2 THE CINDERELLA WINDOW BOX

The pastel shades of 'Cinderella' stocks and 'Turbo' pansies harmonise perfectly. Both plants have a wonderful scent, particularly the stocks.

Site
Sun or partial shade.

Container
Trevis window box complete with plastic liner inserts: 90cm (3ft) long, 15cm (6") wide, 12.5cm (5") deep.

Planting Time
End April to end May.

Looks its Best
May to June.

Ingredients
>   3 stocks *Matthiola incana* 'Cinderella Red'
>   2 stocks *Matthiola incana* 'Cinderella Rose'
>   1 pansy *Viola* 'Turbo Rose'
>   2 pansies *Viola* 'Turbo Wine Bicolour'
>   3 ornamental nettles *Lamium* 'White Nancy'
>   3 pansies 'Turbo White with Blotch'
>   10 litres of compost
>   Drainage material such as small pieces of polystyrene

Method
1 Make sure the drainage holes are free at the base of the liners. Cover with 2.5cm (1") drainage material and add 7.5cm (3") compost.
2 Plant the three 'Cinderella Red' stocks along the back with the two 'Cinderella Rose' stocks in between.
3 Plant the 'Turbo Rose' pansy and one 'Turbo White with Blotch' pansy in the centre with the two 'Turbo Wine Bicolour' pansies on either side.
4 Plant the ornamental nettles along the front with the other 'Turbo with Blotch' pansies at either end.
5 Water the plants. Add more compost if necessary.

Aftercare
Keep the compost moist; check daily in hot weather. Feed

weekly from mid May onwards. Deadhead regularly. Spray for aphids as necessary. Use the ornamental nettles in a summer display; otherwise discard the stocks and pansies after flowering.

3   THE PANSY HANGING BASKET

This is a very lively basket which will give weeks of colour throughout the spring. Other colour combinations would be equally successful. Try an all-white basket, or mix pretty pink bellis daisies with blue pansies.

Site
Sun or partial shade, sheltered.

Container
Erin wire hanging basket: 35cm (14") diameter with a 27.5cm (11") bracket.

Planting Time
March to April.

Looks its Best
April to May.

Ingredients
    8 daisies *Bellis perennis* 'Tasso Red'
    8 violas *Viola* 'Princess Yellow'
    8 pansies *Viola* 'Turbo Yellow with Red Blotch'
    10 litres of compost
    Moss: *see* right
    Circle of plastic about the size of a small dinner plate

Method
1 Line bottom of basket with a generous layer of moss bringing level a third of the way up the sides. Cover with the plastic circle, then add compost.
2 Alternate four bellis daisies and four violas through the wires so that they are resting on top of the moss. Check the roots make good contact with the compost.
3 Tuck moss between each plant, then add more, so that you create a moss wall two thirds of the way up the sides of the basket. Add extra compost.
4 Plant four pansies through the larger gaps near the top of the sides. Interplant with two daisies and two violas where the gaps are smaller. Again check that the roots make good contact with the compost. Add more moss, bringing level just above basket rim – it may sink a bit on watering.
5 Plant top of basket with two daisies and two violas around

the edge. Stagger them to avoid all daisies and all violas being directly above each other. Plant the remaining four pansies slightly nearer the middle. Fill in the gaps with compost. Water well and check the compost level once more.

Aftercare
Keep the compost moist throughout the spring, be prepared to water daily in very warm weather. Give a liquid feed every week from three weeks after planting. Deadhead to keep the plants tidy and to prolong the flowering. Discard plants in late May/early June.

Hanging Basket liners
I continue to use moss as the liner for my hanging baskets. I find it easy to work with and like the look of it when it is made up. Some argue that its use encourages the destruction of natural habitats, so buy it from a licensed source such as Erin 'Linewell with Moss'. You will find it sold in small bags in all the good garden centres. Many alternative liners exist such as foam, coconut fibre, wool and compressed paper; some are even pre-shaped to fit certain size baskets.

4 THE CINERARIA HANGING BASKET

Here is an instant, easy to plant hanging basket. It looks full and bright, and will continue to flower for many weeks.

Site
Don't put the bracket too high. You want to be able to look into it, not up at it. Any aspect, but must be sheltered.

Container
Hanging basket: 30cm (12") in diameter. You will also need a 22.5cm (9") bracket.

Planting Time
April, as soon as the weather warms up.

Looks its Best
From time of planting until end of May.

Ingredients
  3 cinerarias *Senecio × hybridus* (*Cineraria cruenta*) 'Cindy Blue' (2) and 'Cindy Carmine' (1). These are often sold as house plants. Look for compact plants with lots of buds. Choose a slightly bigger plant for the central position.
  2 primroses *Primula vulgaris* 'Europa Yellow'
  2 variegated ivies *Hedera helix* 'Goldchild'
  8 litres of compost
  Moss: *see* page 21
  Plastic lining cut in the shape of a dinner plate

Method (all top planted)
1 Line the basket with a generous thickness of moss: start at the base and bring it well up the sides so that you form a collar above the rim of the basket.
2 Cut four 2.5cm (1") slits in the plastic lining, then put it in place at the bottom of the basket.
3 Cover the base of the lining with 10cm (4") compost.
4 Alternate the blue cinerarias, primroses and ivies around the edge of the basket.
5 Fill in as necessary with more compost and then place the last cineraria in position right in the crown of the basket.
6 Water well. This will be easier if you use a watering can

with a long spout that can get in between the dense foliage
of the cineraria.

Aftercare

Water as necesary to maintain moist compost. Feed with a
liquid fertiliser every two weeks. When the cinerarias have
finished flowering, remove and discard. Replant the primroses and ivies in a shady position in the garden. The moss
and plastic lining may be used again for a summer planting
so leave them intact.

5 MORE COLOURFUL CINERARIAS

Cinerarias are available in a wide range of blues, pinks and russets. Use them with brightly coloured polyanthus to provide an instant spring display.

Site
A terrace, or next to your front door; any aspect.

Container
This is a 37.5cm (15") square Versailles tub, but any medium to large pot or barrel would suit.

Planting Time
Early April as soon as the weather begins to warm up.

Looks its Best
From time of planting until end May.

Ingredients
  3 *Polyanthus* 'Crescendo Lemon Yellow'
  3 Cinerarias *Senecio × hybridus* (*Cineraria cruenta*) 'Cindy Blue' (2) and 'Cindy Carmine' (1). Usually sold as house plants. Look for compact plants with lots of buds
  2 variegated ivies *Hedera helix* 'Goldchild'
  1 golden conifer, at least 42.5cm (17") high, *Cupressus macrocarpa* 'Goldcrest'
  35 litres of compost
  Drainage material such as small pieces of polystyrene
  Plastic sheeting to line the tub

Method
1 The bottom of the tub has moveable wooden slats. Cover these with the plastic sheeting in which six or more 2.5cm (1") slits have been made.
2 Add 10cm (4") drainage material, then cover with compost leaving about 10cm (4") clear at the top.
3 Plant the ivies at the front corners of the tub, and position of cupressus at the centre back.
4 Plant the tallest of the three polyanthus right in front of the cupressus and the other two behind the ivies.
5 Plant the blue cinerarias at each back corner, and plant the pink one in the centre front of the tub.
6 Make sure the container looks well balanced and that all

the plants are firmly in place. Fill any remaining gaps with
compost.
7 Water well.

Aftercare
Keep the tub well watered, particularly in warm spells. After
the plants have finished flowering, discard the cinerarias,
remove the rest of the plants from the tub and replant in a
shady moist spot in the garden. However, if you wish to use
the ivies and the cupressus in a summer display, just add
busy lizzies.

6   THE RANUNCLUS BARREL

Primroses and ranunculus offer a spectacular range of instant colour for late spring containers. Simply mix and match the ones you like best.

Site
Sun or partial shade but it must be sheltered.

Container
Trevis Swap Tub with separate plastic liner: 35cm (14") diameter, 14cm (5½") deep.

Planting Time
April to May.

Looks its Best
April to May.

Ingredients
   5 ranunculus, a mixture of gold, red, pink and white from
     the Accolade series; other colours are also available
   4 primroses *Primula vulgaris*, a mixture of yellow, scarlet,
     rose and blue from the Europa series
   9 litres of compost
   Drainage material such as small pieces of polystyrene

Method
1 Make sure the drainage holes are free at the base of the
  liner. Cover with 2.5cm (1") drainage material and add
  7.5cm (3") compost.
2 Plant one of the ranunculus in the centre then alternate
  the primroses and remaining ranunculus around the edge.
  Fill in any gaps with compost.
3 Water well and firm in the plants. Add more compost if
  necessary.

Aftercare
Keep the compost moist; check daily in hot weather. Feed
weekly from early May onwards. Deadhead regularly. Spray
for aphids if necessary. The plants can be transferred to
the garden after flowering but they are not fully reliable a
second year.

7   THE CLEMATIS BARREL

Clematis 'H. F. Young' is a beautiful large-flowered hybrid which makes an attractive choice to clothe a patio wall or pergola. Introduced by Pennell's Nurseries, it was named after one of the plant managers in the early 1960s.

Site
Sun or shade (although the roots appreciate shade).

Container
Trevis Barrel Planter 37.5cm (15") diameter 42.5cm (17") deep.

Planting Time
Any time, but avoid frosty or snowy weather.

Looks its Best
Mainly May and June, with a few blooms through the summer, then another flush in September. The main flowering is on the previous season's growth while the autumn flowering takes place at the tip of the current season's growth.

Ingredients
   1 *Clematis* 'H. F. Young'
   2 *Saxifraga moschata* 'Peter Pan'
   36 litres of John Innes No 3 soil
   Drainage material such as small pieces of polystyrene

Method
1 Soak clematis roots in water for 15 minutes before planting.
2 Position the barrel next to place where the clematis will grow, either up a wall, on a pergola etc.
3 Cover the base of the barrel with 5cm (2") drainage and then add approximately 10cm (4") compost (*see* 4 below).
4 Carefully remove clematis from pot and position it in the barrel so that it is 15cm (6") below the top of the barrel. This will help prevent clematis wilt.
5 Direct the cane or support towards the wall or pergola to make training easier.
6 Add soil around roots and bring soil level to within 5cm (2") of the rim of the barrel.
7 Plant one saxifrage in front, the other behind the clematis.
8 Water well. Add more soil if the level has sunk a bit.

Aftercare

Keep the soil moist, watering frequently in spring and summer, feeding regularly with liquid feed at the same time. Encourage shoots to twine round trellis, wires or whatever supports you are offering; growth should reach 2–3m (6–9ft).

Prune the first spring after planting or, if you are planting in spring, right back to within 15–20cm (6–8") of soil level, to a good pair of strong buds. This will encourage valuable growth from the base with lots of flowering potential for future years. Thereafter, prune lightly at end June. Deadhead, with the removal of a few inches of the stem, to encourage autumn flowering. Remove any weak or dead stems. Cut back a few of the main shoots from the base to encourage fresh growth down below. This will help the container look attractive and ensure flowering from top to bottom.

Deadhead the saxifrage in June to keep it tidy. It will soon create a dense mat over the top of the barrel, thereby offering welcome shade to the clematis roots below.

29

HERBS AND VEGETABLES

8 VIOLAS AND PARSLEY

The bright little faces of the 'Johnny Jump Up' violas peep out amongst the parsley. The viola flowers are edible and, of course, so is the parsley. Simple to plant and easy to look after.

Site
Sun or partial shade. It could be grown in a conservatory in March and April.

Container
Small terracotta window box: 35cm (14") long, 17.5cm (7") wide, 17.5cm (7") deep.

Planting Time
Autumn or March/April.

Looks its Best
April to June.

Ingredients
   3 violas *Viola* 'Johnny Jump Up'
   2 parsleys *Petroselinum crispum*
   8 litres of compost
   Drainage material such as small pieces of polystyrene

Method
1 Cover the base of the container wth 2.5cm (1") of drainage material and add 5cm (2") compost.
2 Plant the violas in the centre and one at either end.
3 Plant the parsley in between the violas.
4 Fill in the gaps with compost, bringing the level to within 2.5cm (1") of the rim.
5 Water well. Firm in the plants and add more compost if necessary.

Aftercare
Maintain moisture throughout the period but take care never to water in frosty weather. Apply a liquid feed once a

week from April onwards. Use the flowers as much as you like; cropping will encourage more to form. Once the parsley is well established, cut the leaves, using the outer ones first. The parsley can remain in the box throughout the summer and winter. Cut it down in September and then water well to encourage fresh new growth before the winter. It should survive for two years. Replace the violas in mid summer, with basil, dill or nasturtiums.

9   HERBS AND EDIBLE FLOWERS

A feast for the eyes and the table.

Site
Sunny.

Container
Small terracotta window box: 30cm (12") long, 15cm (6") wide, 15cm (6") deep.

Planting Time
February to March.

Looks its Best
April to May.

Ingredients
    1 golden marjoram *Origanum vulgare* 'Aureum'
    1 variegated mint *Mentha rotundifolia* 'Variegata'
    3 pink daisies *Bellis perennis* 'Tasso Rose'
    2 cowslips *Primula veris*
    5 litres of compost
    Drainage material such as small pieces of polystyrene

Method
1 Cover the base of the container with 2.5cm (1") of drainage material and add 5cm (2") of compost.
2 Plant the majoram at one end and the mint at the other end, both at the front of the window box.
3 Plant the daisies behind the marjoram and mint and one in the centre of the box.
4 Plant the two cowslips, at the back of the box, either side of centre.
5 Fill in the gaps with compost, bringing the level to within 2.5cm (1") of the rim. Water well.

Aftercare
Water regularly so that the compost is kept moist at all times. Apply a liquid feed every week from mid April.
  The daisy and cowslip petals may be taken off and scattered on salads or cake icings etc to make attractive garnishes. Use the mint and marjoram leaves for flavourings and also for decorative purposes. Don't be afraid to use the

mint continually, keeping it well clipped; it will survive unabated. In fact, it lasts well into late autumn/early winter, unlike many of the other mints, and so is of particular value then. The marjoram will have pretty pink flowers in July and August which are wonderfully aromatic. Cut the marjoram back by two-thirds before the winter sets in but leave the seedheads for the birds.

Treat the arrangement either as a long-term planting or transfer the cowslips after flowering to a spot in the garden and plant parsley or basil instead. Basil will be a temporary summer resident but parsley could stay throughout the autumn and winter.

10 YELLOW COURGETTES

Both the flowers and the fruit of yellow courgettes make an attractive display in a pot. Here they show up well against blue lobelia.

Site
Sheltered and sunny.

Container
Red plastic pot: 32.5cm (13") in diameter, 27.5cm (11") deep. Any medium to large pot would be appropriate, but red does make a change!

Early Preparation
Sow two seeds under heat in April or early May, one each in a 7.5cm (3") pot, carefully following the instructions on the packet.

   You will only need the stronger of the two plants for this scheme. Three or four plants would provide enough courgettes for a family of four.

Planting Time
End May. Courgettes are susceptible to frost so protect them on cold nights.

Looks its Best
July to September.

Ingredients
    1 yellow courgette *Cucurbita pepo* 'Gold Rush F1 Hybrid'
    ½ strip *Lobelia erinus* 'Cambridge Blue'
    17 litres of compost
    Drainage material such as small pieces of polystyrene

Method
1 Cover the base of the container with 5cm (2") of drainage material and add 20cm (8") compost.
2 Plant the courgette in the centre of the pot.
3 Divide the lobelia and plant around the edge.
4 Water well. Firm in the plants.

Aftercare
Water regularly; in hot weather be prepared to water daily. Apply a liquid feed every week from the middle of July or whenever the courgettes first begin to flower or set fruit. Aphids should not present a problem but if they do, spray with a safe insecticide suitable for fruit and vegetables.

Harvest the exotic yellow flowers so that they can be stuffed in the Italian style of cooking or cut the fruit when it is between 7.5–20cm (3–8") long and then bake or fry. Do not attempt to eat the lobelia as it is poisonous.

At the end of the autumn, discard all the plants.

11 COMPANION PLANTING FOR TOMATOES

Dwarf tomatoes are interplanted with French marigolds and basil as a companion planting scheme to deter whitefly and other aphids. It makes an extremely attractive arrangement which can be cropped for weeks. It adapts well to large barrels and even hanging baskets.

Site
Sunny position outdoors or partially shaded in the conservatory or greenhouse.

Container
Large Olive Tree terracotta window box: 80cm (32") long, 20cm (8") wide, 17.5cm (7") deep.

Early Preparation
Basil, tomatoes and French marigolds can all be purchased as plants in May but dwarf tomato plants might not be on sale. Therefore, try growing all the plants from seed sold by Thompson and Morgan Ltd, London Road, Ipswich, Suffolk IP2 0BA. Look in your local garden centre, or send for their catalogue. Start them off in gentle heat in March according to the instructions on the packet.

Planting Time
End May. Cold nights will damage young tomato plants. Either keep them in the greenhouse or conservatory until the nights warm up or place them in a very sheltered spot outdoors and, if necessary, cover them with a newspaper at night. They can remain in the conservatory or greenhouse all summer as long as they are not subjected to too much direct sunlight.

Ingredients
    4 dwarf tomatoes: varieties 'Sungold' or 'Sweet 100'
    4 French marigolds *Tagetes patula* 'Special' sold by
       Thompson and Morgan Ltd as a companion plant for
       tomatoes
    6 basil plants *Ocimum minimum* with fragrant spicy leaves.
       There are taller forms as well
    20 litres of compost
    Drainage material such as small pieces of polystyrene

4 60cm (2ft) canes and garden string to support the
tomatoes

Method
1 Cover the base of the container with 2.5cm (1") of drainage
  material and add 7.5cm (3") of compost.
2 Space the four tomatoes along the centre of the window
  box surrounded on all sides by alternating basil and
  marigolds. In this way the tomato plants are surrounded
  by a protective ring of basil and French marigolds.
3 Fill in any remaining gaps with compost, bringing the
  level to within 2.5cm (1") of the rim.
4 Water well and add more compost if necessary to regain
  the level.
5 Stake the tomatoes and tie securely as they grow. Once the
  fruit starts to swell the trusses become quite heavy.

Aftercare
Water regularly; this is of paramount importance. Be prepared to do it once or twice a day in hot weather, particularly once the tomatoes have formed. A great deal is being
asked of in a very confined planting space, so food and water

are essential. Apply a liquid feed once a week after the first flower truss has set. Stake the tomatoes with a strong cane and tie securely.

Remove side shoots and cut off large bottom leaves where they threaten the basil and marigolds. Spraying for aphids should not be necessary or should be minimal. However, you must act quickly if they are apparent, using a safe insecticide suitable for fruit or vegetables. Good ventilation will help to keep the plants healthy. If indoors, provide shading.

Pick the tomatoes regularly as they ripen. Slice them up and enjoy them with a sprinkling of chopped basil on top. Together they make a wonderful treat in high summer.

You could bring the window box inside the greenhouse at the end of summer to allow the last tomatoes to ripen. Otherwise use the green ones for chutney or allow them to ripen indoors on a window still. Remove all the basil leaves and mix with breadcrumbs for a provençale mixture. Freeze and enjoy it throughout the winter. Discard the French marigolds but keep some of the seeds for next year.

12   RUNNER BEANS AND SWEET PEAS

Old-fashioned sweet peas make a lovely scented pillar which can be used for cut flowers from June to September. Combine them with runner beans and you have the double advantage of flowers for the house and beans for the table.

Site
Sheltered; sun or partial shade.

Container
Large, deep pot or wooden barrel: 45cm (18") in diameter, 30cm (12") deep.

Early Preparation
Sweet pea 'Antique Fantasy' is very fragrant. The seed is available from Thompson and Morgan Ltd (*see* page 36). (Of course, there are other sweetly-scented sweet peas available as well but do be careful as not all sweet peas have a strong scent.) In March sow two seeds each to four 7.5cm (3") pots.

Planting Time
May. Runner beans will be killed by frost so give protection on cold nights.

Ingredients
- 4 sweet pea plants (8 seeds); remove the weaker of each pair. *Lathyrus odoratus* 'Antique Fantasy'. There is a lovely range of colours and good long stems for cutting
- 4 white-flowering runner bean plants (8 seeds) *Phaseolus coccineus* 'Desiree'; a very productive stringless variety
- 32 litres of compost

Drainage material such as broken bricks or clay crocks to add weight to the bottom of the container and so prevent the planting being blown over in the wind. In addition finer drainage material to go on top

8 2.4m (8ft) canes plus garden string or wire to draw them into a circle at the top

Method
1 Cover the base of the container with 7.5cm (3") of heavy drainage material. Then cover with a shallow layer of fine pieces.
2 Add sufficient compost to bring the level to within 2.5cm (1") of the rim of the container.
3 Alternate the four sweet pea plants and the four runner beans around the outside of the container to form a wide circle. The runner beans can be sown direct at this stage (sow four groups of two beans and remove the weakest once they have germinated).
4 Water well. Firm in the plants and place the canes near to each one. Tie the wire or string to each one near the top of the canes so that they will give each other support.

Aftercare
Pinch out the growing tips of the sweet pea plants when they are 10cm (4") high to encourage lateral shoots. Pinch out the growing tips of the runner beans when they have reached the top of the canes.

Keep the container well watered throughout the growing season; be prepared to water daily in hot weather. Turn the pot around regularly to allow the sun to reach all sides. The sweet peas should attract the bees and help pollinate the beans. If attacked by aphids use an insecticide suitable for vegetables and which will not harm bees. Apply a liquid feed every two weeks from end June.

Be careful to remove all seed pods on the sweet peas to encourage further flowering. Better still, cut the flowers and so enjoy their fragrance inside. New buds will soon open and that way you will get an abundant crop.

Crop the beans as soon as they are long enough. Take them while young and tender to encourage further production.

At the end of the autumn, discard all the plants.

13 A GREEN PEPPER POT

Green peppers and colourful French marigolds make an attractive pot for a sunny patio or conservatory.

Site
Sunny and sheltered patio or porch, greenhouse or conservatory.

Container
Clay pot: 27.5cm (11") in diameter, 25cm (10") deep.

Early Preparation
Both the pepper and the French marigolds may be grown from seed, starting them off in March. They can also be bought from garden centres in May. Three pepper plants should provide a good crop for a family of four.

Planting Time
End May to early June.

Looks its Best
It will crop August to September.

Ingredients
   1 green pepper *Capsicum annuum*; 'Gypsy F1 Hybrid' from Thompson and Morgan Ltd (*see* page 36) would be a suitable one for the south, while 'Canape F1 Hybrid' would be more suitable for northern areas
   2 French marigolds *Tagetes patula* 'Special', a Thompson and Morgan Ltd companion plant to deter whitefly and other aphids
   10 litres of compost
   Drainage material such as small pieces of polystyrene
   1 90cm (3ft) cane for support

Method
1 Cover the base of the container with 5cm (2") of drainage material and add sufficient compost to bring the level up to within 5cm (2") of the rim of the pot.
2 Plant the pepper at the centre-back of the pot with the French marigolds on either side of the front.
3 Bring the compost level to within 2.5cm (1") of the rim of the container. Water well.

4 Fix the cane so that it will give support as the pepper plant
grows.

Aftercare
Maintain compost moisture throughout the summer. Apply
a liquid feed weekly once the peppers have begun to set fruit.
Under glass, shade in very hot weather; here red spider may
be a problem. Whitefly and greenfly should be kept at bay
by the French marigolds, but spray with a safe vegetable
insecticide if necessary. Keep cropping the peppers as soon
as they are big enough to eat to encourage further production. Deadhead the French marigolds.

At the end of the summer, discard all the plants.

SUMMER HANGING BASKETS

14 A BALL OF BUSY LIZZIES

This is a good basket for sun or shade and the colours can
be varied to suit yourself. It is easy to look after.

Site
It will enjoy the sun and tolerate quite deep shade.

Container
Wire hanging basket: 30cm (12") in diameter, with a sturdy
22.5cm (9") bracket.

Planting Time
Mid May to early June.

Looks its Best
Mid June onwards.

Ingredients
> 9 busy lizzies *Impatiens* including 'Accent Pink', 'Accent
> Carmine', 'Accent Rose' and 'Accent White'. These are
> all excellent colours which look good together
> 2 strips of trailing *Lobelia erinus* 'String of Pearls'
> 8 litres of compost
> Moss; *see* page 21
> A circle of plastic about the size of a saucer

Method
1 Line the basket with a generous thickness of moss, starting at the base and working one third of the way up the
   sides.
2 Place the plastic circle and place over the moss lining in
   the bottom of the basket. Add 5cm (2") compost.
3 Divide one strip of lobelia and, planting from the outside
   of the basket inwards, pass the roots between the wires so
   that they make good contact with the compost. Continue
   round the basket.
4 Add another ring of moss making sure that there are no
   gaps around the lobelia plants.
5 Plant four busy lizzies at regular intervals around the front

and sides of the basket (only avoid the back as this will be against the wall).

6 Add another ring of moss, bringing it right to the top so that it forms a good thick collar 2.5cm (1") above the rim of the basket. Add more compost.

7 Plant remaining busy lizzies in the top of the basket.

8 Divide the second strip of lobelia and plant around the rim so that it will trail over the sides.

9 Water carefully but well. Add more compost and moss if necessary.

Aftercare

Water generously. In hot weather you must be prepared to do it daily. Your aim is to get the whole basket thoroughly wet so that the moss is wet to touch all the way round. Once a week give the plants a liquid feed. At the end of summer dismantle the basket and discard all the plants.

15   A SMALL BEGONIA BASKET

Here's an idea for a small ball-shaped basket where young plants can be bought in polystyrene strips or cells. The begonia flowers have bright yellow stamens surrounded by glistening white petals. The colour combination is repeated in the white lobelia and yellow marigolds. The result is both refreshing and unusual.

Site
Sun or shade. Also effective when placed on top of a chimney pot.

Container
Erin wire hanging basket: 30cm (12") diameter, with a 22.5cm (9") bracket.

Planting Time
Mid May to early June.

Looks its Best
Mid June to September.

Ingredients
   12 upright *Lobelia erinus* 'White Lady'
   12 fibrous rooted *Begonia semperflorens* 'Olympia White'
   4 French marigolds *Tagetes patula* 'Aurora Light Yellow'
   8 litres of compost
   Moss; *see* page 21
   Circle of plastic sheeting the size of a saucer

Method
1 Line the base of the basket with moss, bringing it a third of the way up the sides. Place the plastic circle over the moss lining and add compost to the level of the moss.
2 Alternate four lobelia and four begonias to form a circle through the wires. Check the roots make good contact with the compost.
3 Tuck moss between each plant then bring the moss wall two thirds of the way up the sides of the basket. Add extra compost.
4 Alternate five lobelia and five begonias with a marigold for the centre front. Stagger the planting so that, where

possible, a begonia is above a lobelia or vice versa. Check
the roots make good contact with the compost.
5 Again tuck moss between each plant and then bring level
  just above rim of basket (it will sink slightly on watering).
6 Plant the top of basket with the final three marigolds, three
  begonias and three lobelia. Fill in the gaps with compost.
7 Water well. Add more moss and compost as necessary.

Aftercare

Keep the compost moist at all times, check daily in hot
weather.

Give a liquid feed every week from the end of June.
Deadhead the begonias and marigolds. Discard the plants
in the autumn.

16   A BASKET OF ZANY GAZANIAS

Gazanias and French marigolds make good partners. They are both available in shades of yellow, gold and orange with bronze tonings and they both love to bask in the sun. Here, crinkly parsley fills the gap between the top and sides.

Site
Full sun.

Container
Erin wire hanging basket: 35cm (14") diameter, with a 27.5cm (11") bracket. Position at eye level or below so that you can really appreciate the gazanias.

Planting Time
Mid May to early June.

Looks its Best
Mid June to September.

Ingredients
   8 French marigolds *Tagetes patula* 'Alamo Orange'
   4 French marigolds *Tagetes patula* 'Alamo Gold'
   4 French marigolds *Tagetes patula* 'Alamo Harmony', a maroon and gold bicolour
   6 parsleys *Petroselinium crispum*
   3 *Gazania splendens* 'Daybreak Bronze'
   3 *Gazania splendens* 'Daybreak Yellow'
  10 litres of compost
   Moss; *see* page 21
   Circle of plastic sheeting the size of a saucer

Method
1 Line the base of the basket with moss bringing it a third of the way up the sides. Place the plastic circle over the moss in the base of the basket. Add a layer of compost.
2 Plant a mixture of eight marigolds through the wires to form a circle near the base of the basket. Check the roots make good contact with the compost.
3 Tuck moss between each plant then bring the moss wall two thirds of the way up the sides of the basket. Add extra compost.
4 Alternate eight more marigolds with three of the parsley

plants. Again, check the roots make good contact with the compost. Tuck moss between each plant and then bring level just above rim of basket (it will sink slightly on watering).

5 Now plant the top of the basket. Stagger the remaining parsley plants around the edge. Try to arrange them so that they are planted above a marigold (not another parsley). This way they will form a frill between sides and top.

6 Plant the gazanias in the centre and spaced out around the sides. Fill in the gaps with compost.

7 Water well. Add more moss and compost as necessary.

Aftercare

Keep the compost moist at all times, check daily in hot weather. Give a liquid feed every week from the end of June. Deadhead the gazanias and marigolds and feel free to crop the parsley. The gazanias can be overwintered, *see* page 14; discard the other plants.

17   A BASKET OF CANDY PINKS AND BLUES

Here is a basket bursting with a host of richly coloured lobelias. They are all upright varieties which results in a more compact basket. Trailing lobelias could easily be used instead but the effect would be quite different. There are several different shades of blue to choose from.

Site
Sun or partial shade.

Container
Erin wire hanging basket: 35cm (14") diameter, with a 27.5cm (11") bracket.

Planting Time
Mid May to early June.

Looks its Best
Mid June to September.

Ingredients
    4 upright *Lobelia erinus* 'Blue Sky'
    2 upright *Lobelia erinus* 'Riviera Sky Blue'
    2 upright *Lobelia erinus* 'White Lady'
    6 upright *Lobelia erinus* 'Riviera Blue Splash'
    5 busy lizzies *Impatiens* 'Accent Rose Star'
    1 upright pink geranium *Pelargonium* 'Century Rose'
    2 upright pink *Verbena hortensis* 'Amour Rose'
    1 bush pink *Fuchsia* 'Miss California'
    2 trailing ivy-leaf pink geraniums *Pelargonium* 'Pico'
    10 litres of compost
    Moss; *see* page 21
    Circle of plastic sheeting the size of a saucer

Method
1 Line the base of the basket with moss bringing it a third of the way up the sides. Place the plastic circle over the moss in the base of the basket. Add a layer of compost.
2 Alternate four lobelia 'Blue Sky' and four busy lizzies through the wires to form a circle near the base of the basket. Check the roots make good contact with the compost.

3 Tuck moss between each plant then bring the moss wall two-thirds of the way up the sides of the basket. Add extra compost.

4 Plant five more lobelias in a wide circle around the basket including 'Riviera Sky Blue' and 'White Lady' near the front. Again, check the roots make good contact with the compost. Tuck moss between each plant and then bring level just above rim of basket (it will sink slightly on watering). Add more compost.

5 Now plant the top of the basket. Plant the 'Century' geranium in centre back position with the verbenas on either side.

6 Plant the remaining busy lizzie in the centre.

7 Plant the fuchsia at the front of the basket with the two trailing geraniums on either side. Plant the remaining lobelia in any gaps around the edge.

8 Water well. Add more moss and compost as necessary.

Aftercare

Keep the compost moist at all times, check daily in hot weather. Give a liquid feed every week from the end of June. Deadhead regularly. Spray if necessary. The geraniums and fuchsia can be overwintered, *see* page 14; discard the other plants.

18 A BASKET OF ICY PETUNIAS AND HOT MEXICANAS

This soon creates a dazzling display, with its attractive stripes and frills.

Site
Sunny.

Container
Wire hanging basket: 35cm (14") in diameter, with a sturdy 27.5cm (11") bracket.

Planting Time
Mid May to early June.

Looks its Best
From time of planting until end September.

Ingredients
    2 strips of trailing *Lobelia erinus* 'White Lady'
    4 trailing ivy leaf geraniums *Pelargonium* 'Mexicana'
    2 silver leaf cinerarias *Senecio cineraria* (*Cineraria maritima*)
    3 *Petunia* 'Blue Ice'
    2 *Petunia* 'Rose Ice'
    10 litres of compost
    Moss; *see* page 21
    Circle of plastic cut about the size of a saucer

Method
1 Line the basket with a generous thickness of moss, starting at the base and working up the sides so that you form a collar above the rim of the basket.
2 Place the plastic circle over the moss lining in the bottom of the basket and add 7.5cm (3") compost.
3 Divide the strips of lobelia, and plant a circle around the middle of the basket. Starting from the outside of the basket inwards, pass the roots through a hole you have a made in the moss so that they make good contact with the compost. Close the gap in the moss and continue round the basket.
4 Plant one 'Blue Ice' petunia in the centre top of the basket surrounded by the other four petunias and cinerarias.

5 Plant the geraniums around the edge of the basket, two at the front and two at the sides. Avoid the back as that will be hidden against the wall.
6 Then plant the second strip of lobelia in between the geraniums.
7 Make sure that all the plants are firmly in place, filling any remaining gaps with compost.
8 Water well. Add more moss or compost if necessary.

Aftercare

Water generously. In hot weather, be prepared to do it daily. Aim to get the whole basket thoroughly wet to the touch all the way round. Once a week give a liquid feed. Deadhead fading petunia and geranium flowers daily. Spray for greenfly, etc. as a matter of routine once a week. At the end of the summer, dismantle the basket; keep the geraniums (*see* page 14) but discard the rest.

19   A BASKET OF ORANGES

Brilliant oranges and pale pinks are sure to enliven any dull spot.

Site
In full or partial shade.

Container
Wire hanging basket: 35cm (14") in diameter, with a sturdy 27.5cm (11") bracket.

Early preparation
See page 14 if you wish to start your own begonia tubers.

Planting Time
Mid May to early June

Looks its Best
It should begin to look good from mid June onwards

Ingredients
    1 strip upright *Lobelia erinus* 'Mrs Clibran'
    1 medium *Begonia* × *tuberhybrida* 'Nonstop Orange Improved'
    3 trailing *Begonia* × *tuberhybrida* 'Finale Orange'
    1 *Fuchsia* 'Orange Drops'
    3 busy lizzies *Impatiens* 'Accent Pink' (or 'Salmon')
    2 wandering jews *Tradescantia albiflora*
  10 litres of compost
    Moss; *see* page 21
    Circle of plastic about the size of a saucer

Method
1 Line the basket with a generous thickness of moss, starting at the base and working up the sides so that you form
a collar above the rim of the basket.
2 Place the plastic circle over the moss lining in the bottom
of the basket. Add 7.5cm (3") compost.
3 Divide the strip of lobelia. Make a hole in the moss in the
centre of the basket and planting from the outside of the
basket inwards, pass the roots through the moss until they
make good contact with the compost. Close the gap in the
moss and continue round the middle of the basket.

4 At the top of the basket, plant the largest of the three trailing begonias at the front of the basket, leave a gap and then plant the other two on either side.

5 Plant the fuchsia in the middle and the non-stop begonia towards centre back.

6 Plant the three busy lizzies behind the trailing begonias.

7 Tuck the tradescantia between the busy lizzies.

8 Make sure all the plants are firmly in place, filling any remaining gaps with compost.

9 Water well. Add more compost or moss if necessary.

Aftercare

Water daily in hot weather, at soil level, otherwise the water will run off the begonia leaves and not soak in. Once a week give a liquid feed. Spray for greenfly, etc. as necessary and deadhead begonia and fuchsia flowers. At end September, dismantle the basket. Overwinter the fuschsia and begonias (*see* page 14). You can take cuttings of the tradescantia and grow them indoors, but throw the lobelia away.

20   A BASKET OF SIMPLE SURFINIAS

This basket is very easy to make up as it is entirely top planted. Surfinia® petunias and scaevolas make excellent bedfellows. They are both strong growing and together will create a cascade of colour all summer through.

Site
Sun or partial shade. This is suitable for a high bracket as the petunias will trail several feet by the end of the summer.

Container
Erin wire hanging basket: 35cm (14") diameter, with a 35cm (14") bracket. After just two months' growth, the plants in this basket were already 105cm (42") wide!

Planting Time
Mid May to early June.

Looks its Best
Mid June to September

Ingredients
> 1 trailing *Petunia* 'Surfinia Purple Mini'
> 3 *Scaevola aemula* 'Blue Fan'
> 2 trailing *Petunia* 'Surfinia Brilliant Rose'
> 1 trailing *Petunia* 'Surfinia Pink'
> 10 litres of compost
> Moss; *see* page 21
> Circle of plastic sheeting the size of a saucer

Method (all top planted)
1 Line the base of the basket with moss. Create a wall of moss all the way up the sides so that it forms a collar just above the rim of the basket (it will sink slightly on watering).
2 Place the plastic circle over the moss lining in the base of the basket. Add two thirds of the compost.
3 Plant the 'Surfinia Purple Mini' petunia so that it trails over the edge and down the front of the basket.
4 Plant two scaevolas on either side with the third at the back of the basket.
5 Plant the two 'Surfinia Brilliant Rose' petunias on opposite sides in between the scaevolas.

6 Plant the 'Surfinia Pink' petunia in the centre. The colour contrast makes it a good centre piece.
7 Fill in the gaps with compost. Firm in the plants.
8 Water well. Add more moss or compost if necessary.

Aftercare
Keep the compost moist at all times, check daily in hot weather. Give a liquid feed every week from the end of June. This basket should be really easy to look after. Just dead-head the petunias and spray for aphids if necessary. All these plants should be discarded at the end of the summer.

® The name Surfinia is registered.

SUMMER WINDOW BOXES

21 A SUN-LOVING BOX

This is simple to plant, easy to look after but it needs lots of sun to make it look so pretty.

Site
Window ledge; full sun.

Container
Large Olive Tree terracotta window box: 80cm (32") long, 20cm (8") wide, 17.5cm (7") deep.

Planting Time
End May to early June onwards.

Looks its Best
End June to September.

Ingredients
   5 various coloured *Gazania*
   1 strip of Livingstone daisies *Mesembryanthemum criniflorum*
   20 litres of compost
   Drainage material such as small pieces of polystyrene

Method
1 Cover the base of the container with 2.5cm (1") drainage material and add enough compost to bring the level to within 2.5cm (1") of the rim of the box.
2 Plant the gazanias spaced out along the middle of the box.
3 Carefully separate the Livingstone daisies, and plant along the front of the box so that they will spread over the edge.
4 Make sure that all the plants are firmly in place, filling any remaining gaps with compost.
5 Water well. Add more compost if necessary.

Aftercare
This is an easy, generally trouble free box. Water regularly, although the Livingstone daisies prefer to be on the dry side. The gazanias need only an occasional liquid feed (not before

the Livingstone daisies are in flower). But what they both ask for is lots of sun!

At the end of the summer discard the Livingstone daisies and the gazanias unless you wish to try to overwinter the latter, *see* page 14.

22   A BLAZING WINDOW BOX

The combination of red, yellow and blue never fails to catch
the eye. Here is a simple planting that is cheap, cheerful and
easy to look after.

Site
A sunny window ledge.

Container
Medium wooden window box (with a plastic liner): 55cm
(22") long, 15cm (6") wide, 12.5cm (5") deep.

Planting Time
Mid to end May onwards.

Looks its Best
June to September.

Ingredients
  1 strip of upright *Lobelia erinus* 'Mrs Clibran'

1 strip or 6 plants of dwarf single French marigold *Tagetes tenuifolia* 'Lemon Gem'
1 strip or 6 plants of *Salvia splendens* 'Blaze of Fire'
6 litres of compost
Drainage material such as small pieces of polystyrene

Method
1 Cover the base of the container with 2.5cm (1") drainage material and add 7.5cm (3") compost.
2 Alternate the salvias and tagetes in two rows at the front and back of the box.
3 Divide the lobelia and plant along the front edge and sides of the box.
4 Make sure the plants are firmly in place, filling any remaining gaps with compost.
5 Water well. Add more compost if necessary.

Aftercare
Water regularly, and feed once a week. You should not be troubled by greenfly etc., but if they do appear then spray accordingly. At the end of the season, discard all the plants.

23 SOMETHING FOR SHADE

The fuchsias and busy lizzies create a pastel mound together and don't seem to mind their shady home one bit.

Site
A shady window ledge.

Container
Large window box: 85cm (34") long, 20cm (8") wide, 17.5cm (7") deep.

Planting Time
Mid to end May onwards.

Looks its Best
June to late September.

Ingredients
    4 busy lizzies *Impatiens* 'Accent Rose'
    4 busy lizzies *Impatiens* 'Accent Pink'
    2 white *Fuchsia* 'Igloo Maid'.

4 silver leaf cinerarias *Senecio cineraria (Cineraria maritima)*
21 litres of compost
Drainage material such as small pieces of polystyrene

Method
1 Cover the base of the container with 2.5cm (1") drainage material and add 5cm (2") compost.
2 Plant the front of the box from left to right: rose busy lizzie, fuchsia, pink busy lizzie, fuchsia, rose busy lizzie.
3 At the back of the box from left to right plant: pink, rose, pink, rose and then pink busy lizzie.
4 In the centre, space the four silver cinerarias.
5 Make sure that all the plants are firmly in place, filling any remaining gaps with compost. Water well.

Aftercare
These plants are thirsty drinkers and need watering regularly. Feed once a week as soon as the fuchsias begin to flower. Deadhead and spray for greenfly. At the end of the summer, discard the buzy lizzies and cinerarias. *See* page 14 if you wish to keep the fuchsias.

24 SIMPLE BEGONIAS

Begonias are a good subject for a window box. What is more they will thrive even on a north-facing window ledge.

Site
Window ledge with sun or shade.

Container
Medium window box (wooden with a plastic liner): 55cm (22") long, 15cm (6") wide, 12.5cm (5") deep.

Early preparation
If you want to use begonia tubers – they will work out cheaper and you will find a better choice of colour – purchase in February or March at the latest (*see* page 14).

Planting Time
Mid May to early June.

Looks its Best
Mid June until end September.

Ingredients
   3 medium upright *Begonia* × *tuberhybrida* 'Nonstop Pink'
   4 *Coleus blumei*. There are some beautiful pink tinges to the leaf colourings. Choose any which will look good with the begonias
   1 strip of trailing *Lobelia erinus* 'Blue Cascade'
   6 litres of compost
   Drainage material such as small pieces of polystyrene

Method
1 Cover the base of the container with 2.5cm (1") drainage material and add 5cm (2") compost.
2 Space the begonias along the length of the box, if one of them is bigger than the others save it for the centre.
3 Plant two coleus plants at the back of the box so that they can be seen from inside the house, and two at either end.
4 Carefully divide the lobelia and plant around the sides and front of the box.
5 Make sure that all the plants are firmly in place, filling any remaining gaps with compost.
6 Water well. Add more compost if necessary.

Aftercare

The box should be watered regularly, as rain water will not penetrate the large flat begonia leaves which act rather like an umbrella. Use a long-spouted watering can to get between the leaves. Once flowering has begun give the plants a fortnightly liquid feed.

Remove all fading begonia flowers. Nip out the flower spikes of the coleus, and also the leading shoots to keep the plants bushy. By late autumn the begonia leaves will begin to turn yellow. Discard the lobelia and coleus. To over-winter the begonias, *see* page 14.

25 THE PATRIOTIC WINDOW BOX

Red, white and blue makes a striking combination accentuated by the stars on both the busy lizzies and the petunias. As the summer progressed, the red begonias and geraniums became bolder and bolder.

Site
Sun or partial shade.

Container
Trevis window box complete with plastic liner inserts: 90cm (3ft) long, 15cm (6") wide, 12.5cm (5") deep.

Early Preparation
If you want to use begonia tubers – they will work out cheaper and you will find a better choice of colour – purchase in February or March at the latest, *see* page 14.

Planting Time
Mid May to early June.

Looks its Best
June to September.

Ingredients
  3 upright geraniums *Pelargonium* 'Century Scarlet'
  3 *Petunia* 'Frenzy Blue Star'
  2 medium tall *Begonia* × *tuberhybrida* 'Nonstop Bright Red'
  3 busy lizzies *Impatiens* 'Accent Red Star'
  4 upright *Lobelia erinus* 'Mrs. Clibran'
  10 litres of compost
  Drainage material such as small pieces of polystyrene

Method
1 Make sure the drainage holes are free at the base of the liners. Cover with 2.5cm (1") drainage material and add 7.5cm (3") compost.
2 Along the back, plant a geranium at either end with the petunias in between.
3 Plant the third geranium in the centre with the begonias on either side.
4 Alternate the busy lizzies and lobelia along the front.

5 Water and firm in the plants. Add more compost if necessary.

Aftercare
Keep the compost moist; check daily in hot weather. Feed weekly from end June onwards. Deadhead regularly. Spray as necessary. The begonias and geraniums may be over-wintered, *see* page 14; discard the other plants.

26 THE BLUSHING BRIDE

These trailing geraniums gave an outstanding performance as they filled the front of the window box, competing for space with busy lizzy 'Bright Eye'. Both have blush pink colouring and a lovely deep rose centre.

Site
Sun or partial shade.

Container
Trevis window box complete with plastic liner inserts: 90cm (3ft) long, 15cm (6") wide, 12.5cm (5") deep.

Planting Time
Mid May to early June.

Looks its Best
June to September.

Ingredients
    3 *Petunia* 'Frenzy Pink Morn'
    2 *Petunia* 'Frenzy Light Blue'
    3 upright pink geraniums *Pelargonium* 'Century Rose'
    3 trailing geraniums *Pelargonium* 'Blanche'
    6 trailing *Lobelia erinus* 'Blue Fountain'
    2 busy lizzies *Impatiens* 'Accent Bright Eye'
    10 litres of compost
    Drainage material such as small pieces of polystyrene

Method
1 Make sure the drainage holes are free at the base of the liners. Cover with 2.5cm (1") drainage material and add 7.5cm (3") compost.
2 Mix the pink and blue petunias along the back with the three upright pink geraniums spaced along the middle.
3 Alternate the trailing geraniums along the front of the box with the lobelia and busy lizzies.
4 Water and firm in the plants. Add more compost if necessary.

Aftercare
Keep the compost moist; check daily in hot weather. Apply a liquid feed every week from the end of June onwards.

Deadhead the geraniums regularly. Spray for greenfly as necessary. All the geraniums may be overwintered, *see* page 14; discard the lobelia, petunias and buzy lizzies after flowering is over.

SUMMER POTS AND BARRELS

27   STRAWBERRY PARFAIT

'Strawberry Parfait' is a good name for this striking little dianthus which is smothered in flowers throughout the height of the summer. For a larger pot, use the same basic planting scheme, but interplant the dianthus with parsley.

Site
Sun or partial shade.

Container
Kingfisher stone pot 30cm (12") across, 25cm (10") deep.

Planting Time
Mid May to early June.

Looks its Best
June to August.

Ingredients
    1 upright geranium *Pelargonium* 'Century Cardinal'
    3 *Dianthus* 'Strawberry Parfait'
    3 upright *Lobelia erinus* 'White Lady'
    3 upright *Lobelia erinus* 'Mrs Clibran'
    12 litres of compost
    Drainage material such as small pieces of polystyrene

Method
1 Cover the base of the pot with 5cm (2") drainage material and add enough compost to bring the level to within 2.5cm (1") of the rim of the container.
2 Plant the red geranium in the centre surrounded by the three dianthus.
3 Alternate the white with the blue-and-white lobelias, in between the dianthus, around the edge of the pot.
4 Water well. Firm in the plants. Add more compost if necessary.

Aftercare
Keep the compost moist; check daily in hot weather. Feed

weekly from end June onwards. Be sure to deadhead the dianthus and geranium regularly. Spray as necessary. The geranium may be overwintered, *see* page 14; discard the other plants after flowering.

28 THE FUCHSIA PEDESTAL

This simple but graceful partnership of fuchsias, petunias and lime-green helichrysum fully complements the elegant vase and pedestal.

Site
Sun or partial shade.

Container
Kingfisher stone vase 40cm (16") diameter, 35cm (14") high; on a pedestal 32.5cm (13") across, 40cm (16") high.

Planting Time
Mid May to early June.

Looks its Best
June to September.

Ingredients
3 bush *Fuchsia* 'Beacon Rosa'
1 *Helichrysum petiolare* 'Limelight'
2 *Petunia* 'Express Sky Blue'
2 *Petunia* 'Frenzy Pink Morn'
35 litres of compost
Drainage material such as small pieces of polystyrene

Method
1 Cover the base of the vase with 2.5cm (1") drainage material and add enough compost to bring the level to within 5cm (2") of the rim of the container.
2 Space the three fuchsias around the edge of the vase.
3 Plant the helichrysum in the centre surrounded by alternating blue and pink petunias.
4 Fill in the gaps with compost. Water well. Firm in the plants. Check to see that the arrangement is well balanced. Add more compost if necessary.

Aftercare
Keep the compost moist; check daily in hot weather. Feed weekly from end June onwards. Deadhead regularly. Spray for aphids, but be aware that only certain sprays are suitable for fuchsias. Before the first frosts, remove the fuchsias and helichrysum so that they may be overwintered, *see* page 14; discard the petunias.

29 THE PERFECT MATCH

Create a delicate display with this charming new nicotiana
underplanted with a matching shade of petunia whose
flowers stay open all day. Both love the sun. You could also
find petunias to match the beautiful salmon, crimson, red,
pink or white nicotianas which are available as well.

Site
Sun or partial shade.

Container
Kingfisher stone pot 45cm (18") diameter, 25cm (10") deep.

Planting Time
Mid May to early June.

Looks its Best
Mid June to September.

Ingredients
    1 *Helichrysum petiolare* 'Silver'
    3 *Nicotiana alata* 'Havana Appleblossom'
    3 *Petunia* 'Express Light Salmon'
    2 nepeta *Glechoma hederacea* 'Variegata'
    6 upright *Lobelia erinus* 'White Lady'
    28 litres of compost
    Drainage material such as small pieces of polystyrene

Method
1 Cover the base of the pot with 5cm (2") drainage material
  and add enough compost to bring the level to within 2.5cm
  (1") of the rim of the container.
2 Plant the helichrysum in the middle surrounded by
  nicotianas.
3 Plant the petunias in a wider triangle beyond the
  nicotianas.
4 Plant the nepeta on either side of the pot with lobelia
  interplanted round the edge.
5 Water and firm in the plants. Add more compost if
  necessary.

Aftercare
Keep the compost moist at all times, check daily in hot

74

weather. Give a weekly liquid feed from late June onwards.
Deadhead the petunias and nicotianas. Spray as necessary.
Discard the flowering plants in the autumn; both the nepeta
and helichrysum may be overwintered, *see* page 14.

30   VANILLA ICE

Violet-blues and cream look sensationally cool together in this ornamental Terra Perma pot. Marigold 'Vanilla' is a recent introduction which is well worth seeking out. As the season matures the helichrysum becomes more obvious and makes a worthy contribution. The final result is a glorious colour scheme which would look stunning in stone, wood or terracotta containers.

Site
Sun or partial shade.

Container
Terra Perma pot 42.5cm (17") diameter, 35cm (14") deep.

Planting Time
Mid May to early June.

Looks its Best
June to September.

Ingredients
- 1 *Helichrysum petiolare* 'Limelight'
- 2 *Petunia* 'Express Sky Blue'
- 2 trailing blue *Convolvulus mauritanicus*
- 3 American marigolds *Tagetes erecta* 'Vanilla'
- 3 upright *Lobelia erinus* 'Riviera Blue Splash'
- 3 *Ageratum houstonianum* 'Light Blue Champion'
- 39 litres of compost
- Drainage material such as small pieces of polystyrene

Method
1 Make sure the drainage holes are clear at the base of the container. Cover with 5cm (2") drainage material.
2 Add compost to within 2.5cm (1") of the rim of the container.
3 Plant the helichrysum in the centre of the pot, with a petunia and convolvulus on either side. Plant the convolvulus near the edge of the pot so that it will trail over.
4 Plant the marigolds besides the petunias with the lobelia and ageratum near the rim.
5 Water well. Firm in the plants. Add more compost if necessary.

Aftercare

Keep the compost moist at all times, check daily in hot weather. Give a liquid feed every week from end June. Deadhead the marigolds and petunias regularly. If the petunias threaten to overshadow the marigolds, don't be afraid to trim them back. The helichrysum and convolvulus may be overwintered, see page 14; discard all the other plants.

31   A LITTLE POT OF STARRY-EYED GAZANIAS

Just a few plants make this a bright and cheerful pot. Both gazanias and marigolds have several different shades, from light yellow to deep orange so the colour scheme can be much stronger. The planting scheme adapts easily to a window box or hanging basket where white lobelia could be added, or a charming new white trailing plant called bacopa.

Site
Sun.

Container
Terra Perma 'Traditional Pot' 30cm (12") diameter, 25cm (10") high.

Planting Time
Mid May to early June.

Looks its Best
June to September.

Ingredients
>   3 white *Gazania splendens* from the 'Talent' series
>   (others in the series are yellow, gold and bronze)
>   3 French marigolds *Tagetes patula* 'Aurora Light
>   Yellow'
>   12 litres of compost
>   Drainage material such as small pieces of polystyrene

Method
1 Make sure the drainage holes are free at the base of the container. Cover with 5cm (2") drainage material and add 15cm (6") compost.
2 Alternate the gazanias and French marigolds around the pot keeping the marigolds near the edge.
3 Fill in the gaps with compost. Water well. Firm in the plants. Add more compost if necessary.

Aftercare
Keep the compost moist; check daily in hot weather. Apply a liquid feed every week from the last week in June.

Deadhead both the gazanias and tagetes regularly. Spray for aphids as necessary. Dismantle the pot in mid-October. The gazanias may be overwintered, *see* page 14; discard the other plants.

A mass of fiery blooms erupt out of this little chimney pot. Orange and white look excellent together, set off by the green and white foliage of the plectranthus. But the choice is wide open; geraniums, verbenas, begonias and lobelias are all available in a wide variety of colours.

Site
Sun or shade.

Container
Terra Perma chimney pot 45cm (18") high with a planter of 22.5cm (9") diameter and 20cm (8") deep, which fits in the top.

Early Preparation
If you want to use begonia tubers – they will work out cheaper and you will find a better choice of colour – purchase in February or March at the latest; *see* page 14.

Planting Time
Mid May to early June.

Looks its Best
June to September.

Ingredients
   1 trailing *Plectranthus hirtus* 'Variegatus'
   1 upright geranium *Pelargonium* 'Orange Appeal'
   2 medium tall *Begonia* × *tuberhybrida* 'Nonstop Orange Improved'
   2 trailing *Verbena hortensis* 'Cleopatra White'
   2 upright *Lobelia erinus* 'White Lady' or choose a trailing variety
   5 litres of compost
   Drainage material such as small pieces of polystyrene

Method
1 Cover the base of the container with 5cm (2") drainage material and add 10cm (4") compost.
2 Plant the plectranthus at the back of the pot with the geranium in the centre surrounded by the begonias and verbenas.

3 Plant the lobelia on either side near the front of the pot.
4 Fill in the gaps with compost and water well. Firm in the plants. Add more compost if necessary.

Aftercare
Keep the compost moist; check daily in hot weather. Feed weekly from end June. Deadhead regularly. Spray for aphids as necessary. Encourage the plectranthus to flow through the other plants or be supported by a wall if present. The begonias, geranium and plectranthus may be overwintered, *see* page 14; discard the other plants.

33   THE BEGONIA PEDESTAL

Gorgeous begonias fill the bowl and tumble over the edge interspersed with graceful trails of plectranthus. A multitude of colours can be used together including pinks and white, or choose a single colour theme if you prefer. Either way, this container will last well into autumn.

Site
Sun or shade.

Container
Terra Perma 'Newstead pedestal with Bowl': Bowl 45cm (18") diameter, 20cm (8") deep; on pedestal 50cm (20") high. Stabilise the pedestal by filling it with sand or shingle.

Early Preparation
If you want to use begonia tubers – they will work out cheaper and you will find a better choice of colour – purchase in February or March at the latest; *see* page 14.

Planting Time
Mid May to early June.

Looks its Best
June to September.

Ingredients
   5 trailing *Begonia* × *tuberhybrida* including yellow, apri-
     cot, salmon, red, and orange from the 'Finale' range
   5 upright *Lobelia erinus* 'Mrs. Clibran' or use a trailing
     variety
   1 trailing *Plectranthus hirtus* 'Variegatus'
   2 medium tall *Begonia* × *tuberhybrida* 'Nonstop Yellow'
   1 medium tall *Begonia* × *tuberhybrida* 'Nonstop Orange
     Improved'
   20 litres of compost
   Drainage material such as small pieces of polystyrene

Method
1 Make sure the drainage holes are free at the base of the
   bowl. Cover with 5cm (2") drainage material and add
   10cm (4") compost.
2 Space the trailing begonias and lobelia around the edge of

the bowl. Take care to mix the begonia colours where appropriate.

3 Plant the plectranthus in the centre surrounded by the three non-stop begonias.

4 Fill in the gaps with compost; water well. Firm in the plants. Check to see that the arrangement is well balanced.

Aftercare

Keep the compost moist; check daily in hot weather. Feed weekly from end June. Deadhead regularly. The plectranthus and begonias may be overwintered, *see* page 14; discard the lobelia.

34 FUCHSIAS IN A CHIMNEY POT

These fuchsias look very graceful tumbling out of their chimney pot home. This is easy to plant and simple to look after.

Site
In sun or partial shade.

Container
A tall chimney pot with a small plastic or terracotta container which will fit snugly inside. This one is 25cm (10") in diameter, 22.5cm (9") deep.

Planting Time
Mid May to June.

Looks its Best
From time of planting to end September.

Ingredients
> 2 red and white *Fuchsia* 'Swingtime'
> 2 white daisy-like marguerites *Chrysanthemum frutescens*
> 9 litres of compost
> Drainage material such as small pieces of polystyrene

Method
1 Cover the base of the container with 2.5cm (1") drainage material and add 10cm (4") compost.
2 Plant the fuchsias opposite each other, either side of the pot so that the base of the plants are sitting just below the rim of the pot.
3 Plant the two marguerites in the gaps in between the fuchsias.
4 Make sure the container looks well balanced and that all the plants are firmly in place, filling any remaining gaps with compost.
5 Water well. Add more compost if necessary to bring the level to within 2.5cm (1") of the rim.

Aftercare
Fuchsias are thirsty drinkers and need to be watered frequently. Give the pot a liquid feed once a week and at the same time spray against greenfly etc. The marguerites could

suffer from chrysanthemum leaf miner maggots and should be sprayed accordingly.

Deadhead all faded flowers so that the flowering period is lengthened. At the end of September remove the fuchsias from the container and pot into 15cm (6") pots. If you wish to overwinter the fuschias, *see* page 14; discard the marguerites.

35 SUMMER GLORY

This is a traditional summer planting with red geraniums, busy lizzies, lobelia and alyssum. The effect is very bright and cheerful.

Site
Sun or partial shade.

Container
Medium to large pot: 42.5cm (17") diameter and 42.5cm (17") deep.

Planting Time
Mid to end May onwards.

Looks its Best
June to September.

Ingredients
- 1 upright variegated leaf geranium *Pelargonium* 'Caroline Schmidt'
- 4 upright red geraniums *Pelargonium* 'Cabaret'
- 4 busy lizzies *Impatiens* 'Accent Coral'
- 1 strip of white alyssum *Lobularia maritima* 'Little Dorrit'
- 1 strip of pale blue upright *Lobelia erinus* 'Cambridge Blue'
- ½ strip of dark blue upright *Lobelia erinus* 'Crystal Palace'
- 50 litres of compost
- Drainage material such as small pieces of polystyrene

Method
1. Cover the base of the container with 5cm (2") drainage material and add enough compost to bring level to within 7.5cm (3") of the rim.
2. Plant the variegated leaf geranium in the centre.
3. Plant the four red geraniums in a wide circle, alternating each with a busy lizzie.
4. Divide the alyssum and lobelia and plant alternatively around the edge of the container.
5. Gently firm in the plants. Water well, adding more compost if necessary.

Aftercare
Water regularly, especially in hot weather when a daily check should be made. Apply a liquid feed once every two weeks from the end of June. Spray against greenfly etc as necessary.

Deadhead the geraniums. Discard lobelia, alyssum, busy lizzies at the end of the flowering period. If you wish to over-winter the geraniums, *see* page 14.

36 SUMMER DELIGHT

This is simple to plant, and will delight all summer long. The colours can be changed, of course, but the contrast of white and purple petunias is a good one, particularly when seen against the lime green helichrysum which by the end of the summer will have made a lot of growth and will really show off the petunias well.

Site
Sunny.

Container
Medium sized Olive Tree terracotta pot: 35cm (14") in diameter, 30cm (12") deep.

Planting Time
Mid to end May, onwards.

Looks its Best
May or June onwards.

Ingredients
    1 *Helichrysum petiolatum* 'Limelight'
    2 *Petunia* 'Frenzy Velvet'
    2 *Petunia* 'Frenzy White'
    22 litres of compost
    Drainage material such as small pieces of polystyrene

Method
1 Cover the base of the pot with 5cm (2") drainage material and add enough compost to bring the level to within 2.5cm (1") of the rim.
2 Plant the helichrysum in the middle.
3 Plant the four petunias (alternating white and purple) close to the edge so that they make an informal circle.
4 Firm down all the plants well into the compost.
5 Water well. Add more compost if necessary.

Aftercare
Water generously; in hot weather be prepared to do it daily, but it is best done either in the morning or late evening to avoid scorching the leaves. Use a long-spouted watering can without a rose on the end so that you can get in between the

foliage and avoid wetting, and so spoiling, the flowers. Apply a liquid feed every week from end of June.

Deadhead all fading flowers. Greenfly is a problem with petunias. Watch out for it and spray whenever necessary. If you wish to overwinter the helichrysum, *see* page 14; discard the petunias.

37 SPIDER PLANT WALL POT

A simple but attractive idea for a wall pot. Spider plants are often used as house-plants but why not move them outdoors for the summer and enjoy their foliage amongst your favourite geraniums. Here the combination of salmon pink and lime green looks very pleasing.

Site
Sunny.

Container
Terracotta wall pot: 22.5cm (9") long, 17.5cm (7") wide, 17.5cm (7") deep.

Planting Time
Mid to end May onwards.

Looks its Best
From time of planting until end September or later.

Ingredients
  1 spider plant *Chlorophytum comosum* 'Mandaianum'
  2 upright pink geraniums *Pelargonium* 'Cal'
  3 white alyssum (less than ½ strip) *Lobularia maritima* 'Little Dorrit'
  5 litres of compost
  Drainage material such as small pieces of polystyrene

Method
1 Cover the base of the wall pot with 2.5cm (1") drainage material and add 5cm (2") compost.
2 Plant the spider plant in the centre and the two geraniums on either side.
3 Plant the alyssum around the front and sides.
4 Fill in the gaps with compost. Firm in.
5 Water well. Add more compost if necessary.

Aftercare
Water carefully but regularly and in hot weather be prepared to do it daily as wall pots can dry out very quickly. Give a liquid feed once a fortnight from the middle of July. Dead-head the geraniums as needed and spray against aphids if necessary.

As the summer progresses the spider plant should send out little runners which will eventually trail. In the autumn when you are dismantling the pot these can be detached, potted up and brought indoors with the parent plant for the winter. If you wish to overwinter the geraniums, *see* page 14.

38   A BRIDAL WALL POT

This is the simplest of all combinations and could grace any summer wedding whether the style was Victorian or modern. The name of the geranium is 'L'Elegante' and it has been a favourite for the last hundred years. Fortunately, it is still easily available.

Site
Full sun outdoors or in a conservatory.

Container
Terracotta wall pot: 32.5cm (13") wide, 15cm (6") deep. (This is a particularly large pot so scale down the planting if you are using a smaller one.)

Planting Time
Mid to end May onwards.

Looks its Best
June to September.

Ingredients
   3 white trailing ivy-leaved geraniums *Pelargonium* 'L'Elegante'. It has very attractive variegated leaves which turn mauve around the edges when the plant becomes dry
   1 strip of white alyssum *Lobularia maritima* 'Snowdrift'
   7 litres of compost
   Drainage material such as small pieces of polystyrene

Method
1 Cover the base of the container with 2.5cm (1") of drainage material and add 5cm (2") of compost.
2 Plant the three geraniums so that they trail over the rim of the wall pot.
3 Add more compost to bring the level to within 2.5cm (1") of the rim and plant the alyssum all around the wall pot in between the geraniums and in the corners and around the back.
4 Water well. Gently firm in the plants.

Aftercare
The geraniums will survive quite well without too much
92

water but the alyssum would soon wither away, so water regularly; this might mean every day in hot weather. Apply a liquid feed once a week. Deadhead the geraniums. The alyssum may be subject to downy mildew; spray with Zineb. At the end of the summer discard the alyssum. If you wish to overwinter the geraniums, *see* page 14.

39 ELEGANCE WITH FLOWERS

This pot has an elegant shape and lends itself to this wonderful display of geraniums tumbling down over drifts of lobelia which is planted through holes lower down in the pot.

Site
Sun or partial shade, but the sunnier the better.

Container
Terracotta strawberry pot: 22.5cm (9") in diameter, 42.5cm (17") deep.

Planting Time
Mid to late May onwards.

Looks its Best
From time of planting until the frosts.

Ingredients
    3 ivy leaf geraniums *Pelargonium* 'King of Balcon' or any of the 'Cascade' variety
    ½ strip of upright dark blue *Lobelia erinus* 'Crystal Palace'
    14 litres of compost
    Drainage material such as small pieces of polystyrene (or small stones) and plenty of sharp grit

Method
1 Cover the base of the container with 5cm (2") drainage material.
2 Bring the compost level up to the lowest hole and firm down well. Add extra grit.
3 Carefully separate the strip of lobelia, and, planting from the outside in, pass the roots through the holes so that they are resting on compost. Bring compost level to within 10cm (4") of the rim. Again, add extra grit.
4 Plant the three geraniums so that they are trailing over the sides of the pot.
5 Plant the remaining lobelias in the top of the pot between the geraniums.
6 Make sure that all the plants are firmly in place, filling any remaining gaps with compost.

7 Water well but carefully so as to cause minimum spillage.

8 Add more compost if necessary.

Aftercare

Water regularly but with great care until the roots of the lobelia bind the compost together in the holes. Feed every fortnight from the end of June.

Deadhead all faded flowers. At the end of the summer, discard the lobelia. If you wish to overwinter the geraniums, *see* page 14.

LATE SUMMER AND AUTUMN CONTAINERS

40   A POT FOR MID TO LATE SUMMER

You can choose a mixture of colours or just one. Either way this will have bright autumnal colours for many months.

Site
Sunny.

Container
Almost any medium or large pot would be appropriate, this is a 'Florentine Square' Olive Tree terracotta pot: 30cm (12") cubed.

Planting Time
Mid May to July.

Looks its Best
July to end September or October.

Ingredients
    4 dwarf bedding dahlias any mixture of colours
    4 *Coleus blumei*; there are some beautiful different leaf markings to choose from
    20 litres of compost
    Drainage material such as small pieces of polystyrene

Method
1 Cover the base of the container with 5cm (2") drainage material and add enough compost to bring the level to within 7.5cm (3") of the rim.
2 Place one dahlia in each corner and a coleus in between.
3 Add compost around each plant, firm down, and fill any remaining gaps with compost to bring the level to within 2.5cm (1") of the rim.

Aftercare
Water generously. In hot weather you must be prepared to do it daily. Once flowering is well established the pot would

benefit from a weekly occasional liquid feed. Spray for greenfly, blackfly etc. once a week or more often if necessary. Remove all spent dahlia flowers to prevent seedheads forming. Nip out the flower spikes on the coleus plants so that they remain bushy.

Protect plants from early frosts by covering with newspaper at night. After a severe frost, the dahlias will turn black. At this stage, discard the coleus. If you want to overwinter the dahlia tubers, *see* page 14.

41 A POT OF CHRYSANTHEMUMS

A heady display of chrysanthemums is especially welcome
at a time of year when summer plants are fading.

Site
Sunny.

Container
Medium to large pot. This one is an old sea-kale pot turned
upside-down: 37.5cm (15") in diameter, 42.5cm (17") deep.

Early Preparation
Chrysanthemums are available in mid to late summer from
many garden centres but most of them will be hothouse
plants and they will not be hardy. If you want to try hardy
'cushion' chrysanthemums from Thompson and Morgan
Ltd (*see* page 36) order by mid March. Delivery of young
plants is in April. Grow them on according to the instructions supplied with the order and plant in the final container
in July. There is a minimum order of ten plants. Plant the
rest in window boxes, hanging baskets or individually in the
conservatory.

Planting Time
End July onwards.

Looks its Best
End August to early October.

Ingredients
  4 hardy 'cushion' *Chrysanthemum*; two colours, either
    russet and white or russet and gold, *Chrysanthemum*
    'The 1000 Flowers' sold by Thompson and Morgan
    Ltd. Otherwise try hothouse chrysanthemums or white
    cyclamen
  4 *Coleus blumei*; choose the ones with the most interesting
    leaf colourings
  39 litres of compost
  Drainage material such as small pieces of polystyrene

Method
1 Cover the base of the container with 5cm (2") of drainage
  material and add sufficient compost to bring the level so

that it comes three-quarters of the way up the sides.

2 Plant the chrysanthemums with the two colours opposite each other. Plant the coleus in between.

3 Fill in the gaps with compost, bringing the level to within 2.5cm (1") of the rim.

4 Water well.

Aftercare

Water regularly to maintain a moist compost and apply a liquid feed every week from end August. Deadhead the chrysanthemums and pinch out the flower buds on the coleus. If the frost kills the coleus before the chrysanthemums have finished flowering, simply remove the dead foliage – the chrysanthemums will remain unharmed. After the display is over, plant the chrysanthemums in the garden where they will bloom another year.

42 SUBTLE SHADES FOR AUTUMN

Chrysanthemums are excellent container plants for autumn displays and are available in so many colours. Here is a combination of pink chrysanthemums and trailing blue campanula which create a very restful and pleasing picture.

Site
Sunny.

Container
Small to medium wooden window box: 75cm (30") long, 20cm (8") wide, 20cm (8") deep.

Early Preparation
see page 98.

Planting Time
July to early August.

Looks its Best
End August to early October.

Ingredients
   1 *Hebe* 'La Seduisante' with dark green leaves to contrast with the variegated one below
   2 *Hebe* × *andersonii* 'Variegata'. It has lavender flowers in autumn
   2 hardy 'cushion' *Chrysanthemum* 'The 1000 Flowers' sold by Thompson and Morgan Ltd, (*see* page 36). Otherwise try the hothouse chrysanthemums or pink cyclamen
   3 blue trailing *Campanula isophylla*.
   2 *Sedum sieboldii* 'Medio-variegatum', a trailing foliage plant with fleshy grey and creamy yellow leaves
   23 litres of compost
   Drainage material such as small pieces of polystyrene

Method
1 Cover the base of the container with 2.5cm (1") of drainage material and add 7.5cm (3") of compost.
2 Plant the plain dark green hebe in the centre-back of the box with the two variegated hebes spaced on either side.

3 Plant the two pink chrysanthemums in the middle of the box, either side of the central hebe.
4 Along the front edge of the box, plant the three campanulas with the two sedums in between.
5 Fill in the gaps with compost, bringing the level to within 2.5cm (1") of the rim of the box.
6 Water well. Add more compost if necessary.

Aftercare
Water regularly to maintain a moist compost and apply a liquid feed every week. Deadhead the chrysanthemums, hebes and campanulas. Spray if necessary. At the end of the flowering season remove the chrysanthemums and plant in the garden so that they can be enjoyed another year. Pot up the campanulas and sedums and overwinter in a greenhouse. Leave the hebes in place but plant yellow pansies and pink bellis daisies along the front for a winter and spring display. Put the window box in a sheltered sunny place and with luck the hebes should survive.

43 JUST FOR AUTUMN

This arrangement provides an unusual combination.

Site
Sheltered as possible.

Container
Urn: 30cm (12") in diameter, 22.5cm (9") deep.

Planting Time
Early September to early October.

Looks its Best
From time of planting until first sharp frost: in a sheltered urban area in the south, this could be as late as Christmas.

Ingredients
  1 variegated shrub such as *Hebe × andersonii* 'Variegata'; choose one with plenty of flower spikes
  1 *Hebe* 'La Seduisante', with dark green leaves and violet-blue flowers.
  1 winter cherry *Solanum capsicastrum* 'Covent Garden'
  1 pot plant, *Cyclamen persicum* 'Perfection White'
  12 litres of compost
  Drainage material such as small pieces of polystyrene

Method
1 Cover the base of the container with 2.5cm (1") drainage material and add 10cm (4") compost.
2 Plant the 'La Seduisante' hebe centre back, the variegated hebe centre left, and the solanum centre right.
3 Make sure the container looks well balanced and that all the plants are firmly in place.
4 Insert an empty plant pot in the centre front position and fill in all the gaps with compost.
5 Water well. Add more compost if necessary to bring the level to within 2.5cm (1") of the rim.
6 Remove the empty plant pot and plant the cyclamen last; *see* page 113.

Aftercare
Keep compost moist throughout the autumn but be aware that the needs of the hebes and solanum are greater than that

of the cyclamen. Never water in frosty conditions. It is likely that the cyclamen and then the solanum will die if there is a very sharp frost, although they will withstand much colder conditions than is generally supposed. To prolong the display, protect the plants with a covering of newspaper at night if frost threatens.

The rest of the plants should survive all but the worst winters. Keep them in the container as part of a spring display, replacing the cyclamen and solanum with a primrose and a pot of dwarf daffodills.

44 AUTUMN THYME

Combine golden thyme with pretty violas and bellis daisies to create colour and interest right through to next May.

Site
Sun or partial shade, sheltered.

Container
Kingfisher stone pot 32.5cm (13") across, 25cm (10") deep.

Planting Time
September to October.

At its Best
Autumn to May, except during severe weather.

Ingredients

3 violas *Viola* 'Princess Deep Purple'
2 violas *Viola* 'Princess Yellow'
2 pink daisies *Bellis perennis* 'Pomponette Rose'
3 golden thymes *Thymus* 'Archer's Gold'
15 litres of compost
Drainage material such as small pieces of polystyrene

Method

1 Cover the base of the pot with 5cm (2") drainage material and add enough compost to bring the level to within 2.5cm (1") of the rim of the container.
2 Plant a purple viola in the centre and then arrange the remainder of the plants around the edge of the pot.
3 Water well. Firm in the plants. Add more compost if necessary.

Aftercare

Place the pot where it is sheltered from the north and east winds. In severe weather, give it the protection of a garage or put it besides the house wall surrounded by sacking. Keep the compost moist throughout the autumn, winter and spring, but never water in frosty conditions. Give a liquid feed in late September and again every fortnight from early March until the violas and daisies have finished flowering. In late May transfer the thymes to another pot or into the garden; discard the other plants.

45 NORTHERN LIGHTS

Ornamental kales are superb candidates for containers. Creamy veins thread through the leaves which vary from pale pink to the deepest burgundy. As the nights become colder, the colour intensifies. Then, after a sharp frost, the crinkly tips will glisten and gleam. Surround them with winter-flowering pansies which come in a glorious range of colours.

Site
Sun or partial shade; sheltered.

Container
Terra Perma 'Traditional Planter': 75cm (30") long; 30cm (12") wide and deep.

Planting Time
September to October.

Looks its Best
Autumn through to May, except for severe spells.

Ingredients
1 ornamental kale 'Northern Lights Pink'. Choose a large specimen for the centrepiece of the container
2 ornamental kales 'Northern Lights Rose'
3 winter-flowering pansies *Viola* 'Universal Plus White'
2 winter-flowering pansies *Viola* 'Universal Plus Light Blue'
2 variegated ivies *Hedera helix* 'Golden Gate'
45 litres of compost
Drainage material such as small pieces of polystyrene

Method
1 Make sure the drainage holes are free at the base of the container. Cover with 7.5cm (3") drainage.
2 Add enough compost to bring the level two-thirds of the way up the sides of the container.
3 Plant the 'Northern Lights Pink' kale towards the centre back of the planter, add extra compost along the back then plant two white pansies on either side.
4 Plant the deeper coloured 'Northern Lights Rose' kales towards the front left and right of the container.

5 Add extra compost in the middle and front of the planter. Then plant the third white pansy at the centre front with the two ivies trailing on either side and the two blue pansies behind.

6 Water well. Firm in the plants Add more compost as necessary to bring level to within 2.5cm (1") of the rim of the container.

Aftercare

Place the planter in a sheltered spot, and in very severe conditions offer extra protection by moving it into a garage or keeping it close to a house wall. Keep the compost moist, but never water in frosty weather. Remove dead leaves from the bottom of the ornamental kales. You may like to substitute the kale with polyanthus in early spring. Feed every fortnight from early March. Discard plants at the end of May although, if used, the polyanthus can be transferred to a shady spot in the garden.

46   A BARREL OF DAHLIAS

Dahlias create a marvellous show in tubs where they can spread out and exhibit their brilliant flowers. They are good for a late summer display, adding a new dimension of colour and form.

Site
Sunny.

Container
Wooden half-barrel traditionally painted. To preserve the wood use a plastic pot to fit inside the barrel; this one is 40cm (16") in diameter, 30cm (12") deep.

Early Preparation
To save money and if you want a particular named variety, buy the tubers in February or March when they are available in the garden centres and start into growth by mid April, placing them 10cm (4") deep in dry peat. Once they have started into growth, water them gently. Or buy them in growth from a garden centre in May.

Planting Time
Outdoors, mid to end May onwards.

Looks its Best
July to September or October.

Ingredients
    3 bedding *Dahlia* 'Little William'
    1 mature ivy *Hedera helix* 'Eva'
    ½ strip of upright *Lobelia erinus* 'White Lady'
    28 litres of compost
    Drainage material such as small pieces of polystyrene

Method
1 Cover the base of the plastic liner or barrel with 5cm (2") of drainage material and add sufficient compost to bring the level about halfway up the barrel.
2 Plant the dahlia tubers resting on the compost with their sprouting growths spaced so as to encourage a well-balanced display. Cover gently with compost.
3 Plant the ivy at the front of the barrel.

4 Add more compost to bring the level to within 2.5cm (1")
  of the rim of the container and add the white lobelia
  around the edge. Water well.

Aftercare
Water regularly; this needs to be done daily in hot weather.
Apply a liquid feed once a week from early July. Deadhead
the dahlias to encourage further flowerings and to keep the
display tidy. Destroy any earwigs which appear.

Protect plants from early frosts by covering with newspaper at night. After a severe frost, the dahlias will turn
black. Then, a week later, cut the stems to within 15cm (6")
of compost level. Remove and place the tubers upside-down
for a week to allow moisture to drain out of the hollow stems.
Then put them, stem up, in a box of barely moist peat so
that the peat surrounds them but does not cover their
crowns. Store in a frost-free place at a temperature of 5°C
(41°F). Start into growth into the spring.

Use the ivy for a winter display. Discard the lobelia.

47 AUTUMN GLORY, SPRING CHARM

The same basic planting can create a wonderful picture in both autumn and spring. The greenery and bulbs remain all winter; only the cyclamen disappear, to be replaced by pink primroses.

Site
Ideal for a town basement, or sheltered terrace; any aspect is appropriate although the sunnier the better.

Container
Olive Tree terracotta pedestal and bowl. Pedestal: 52.5cm (21") high; bowl: 52.5cm (21") in diameter, 20cm (8") deep.

Planting Time
Early September to mid October.

Looks its Best
The cyclamen will flower from the time of planting until the first sharp frost. A covering of newspaper at night will help prolong their display. Replace them by primroses in early spring, after which the scillas will begin to flower. The bulb display should be at its best in mid April.

Ingredients
  1 upright heather *Erica arborea* 'Albert's Gold'
  2 *Hebe* × *andersonii* 'Variegata'; choose ones with plenty of flower buds
  2 variegated ivies *Hedera helix* 'Sagittifolia Variegata'
  10 white daffodils *Narcissus triandrus* 'Thalia'
  4 white hyacinths *Hyacinthus orientalis* 'L'Innocence'
  25 blue scillas or squills *Scilla sibirica* 'Spring Beauty'
  4 pot-plant *Cyclamen persicum* 'Perfection Pink'; choose ones with erect sturdy foliage and plenty of flower buds
  4 pink primroses *Primula vulgaris*. Ones from the 'Husky' range would be excellent
  32 litres of compost
  Drainage material such as small pieces of polystyrene

Method
  1 Cover the base of the container with 2.5cm (1") drainage material and add 5cm (2") compost.

2 Plant the hebes to the centre right and centre left of the bowl with the heather immediately behind.

3 Plant the two ivies so that they trail over the rim of the bowl on either side of the hebes.

4 Insert four empty pots, one behind the heather, one between each hebe and ivy, and the fourth near the front rim of the bowl, to mark the position of the four cyclamen.

5 Plant the daffodil and hyacinth bulbs in a narrow arc between the heather and the hebes.

6 Lightly cover with compost until just the tips of the bulbs are showing.

7 Plant the scillas all around the bowl, mainly concentrating on the outer area. Firm them down gently and bring the compost to within 2.5cm (1") of the container rim.

8 Make sure that all the plants are firmly in place, filling any remaining gaps with compost.

9 Water well. Add more compost if necessary to return the level to within 2.5cm (1") of the rim.

10 Remove the empty pots and plant the cyclamen, taking care that their roots sit well down in the container. This avoids getting compost over the centre of the plant which would then become wet when watered. Cyclamen don't like being kept damp around the top of the corm.

Aftercare

Maintain compost moisture throughout the autumn and winter, but avoid direct watering on the cyclamen as their needs are well below average. Never water in frosty conditions.

When the cyclamen have been hit by the frost, remove them, and replace in early spring with four pink primroses. After the bulbs have finished flowering they may be planted out in the garden. Make sure, however, that they have adequate moisture until the leaves die down naturally in June or July.

The hebes may be used for another display in the autumn, and, like the bulbs, they can be lifted from the container and planted out in the garden. Trim the hebes back to within 7.5cm (3") of the base to encourage the plants to make new shoots and remain bushy around the bottom. The heather and ivies may be replanted in the container as part of a summer display.

AUTUMN, WINTER AND SPRING WINDOW BOXES AND HANGING BASKETS

48   SIMPLICITY IN EARLY SPRING

This display is one of the easiest to plant and is sure to give several weeks of lovely fresh colour. The large white flowers of the crocus will open towards the end of March joined by the graceful blooms of 'February Gold'.

Site
Window ledge, with some sun.

Container
Medium terracotta window box: 45cm (18") long, 17.5cm (7") wide, 17.5cm (7") deep.

Planting Time
Early September to early October.

Looks its Best
March through to early April.

Ingredients
   2 variegated ivies *Hedera helix* 'Kolibri'. This has a lot of
      white in its variegation but any variegated ivy would be
      attractive
   10 early dwarf daffodils *Narcissus cyclamineus* 'February
      Gold'
   20 Dutch white *Crocus vernus* 'Jeanne d'Arc'
   10 litres of compost
   Drainage material such as small pieces of polystyrene

Method
1 Cover the base of the container with 2.5cm (1") of drainage
   material and add 5cm (2") compost.
2 Position the ivies at the two front corners of the
   box.
3 Place the daffodil bulbs in two rows towards the back of

the box, avoiding contact either with each other or with the sides of the container.

4 Cover bulbs with compost until just the tips are showing.
5 Now place the crocus corms around the daffodil bulbs and along the front of the box. Firm them gently into the compost.
6 Top up with more compost to bring the level to within 2.5cm (1") of the rim.
7 Water well, adding more compost as is necessary to regain the former level.

Aftercare

Keep compost moist throughout the autumn, winter and particularly in the spring, but never water in frosty conditions.

After the crocuses and daffodils have finished flowering they may be planted out in the garden: take care, however, to minimize root disturbance and make sure that they do not dry out until the leaves die down naturally in June or July. The ivies may be used for another display in the autumn, and may also be planted out in the garden.

49 SOFTNESS AND SCENT

The three bulbs echo the pattern on the window box. The delicate colour of the hyacinths is enhanced by the dainty white arabis. The fragrance from the hyacinths is an additional attraction.

Site
Window ledge; any aspect.

Container
Small terracotta window box: 35cm (14") long, 17.5cm (7") wide, 17.5cm (7") deep.

Planting Time
Early September to mid October.

Looks its Best
The arabis should begin to flower in March; the hyacinths will bloom in early to mid April.

Ingredients
> 3 *Hyacinthus orientalis* 'Gypsy Queen'
> 2 white *Arabis caucasica* 'Snowflake'
> 8 litres of compost
> Drainage; small pieces of polystyrene

Method
1 Cover the base of the container with 2.5cm (1") drainage material and add 5cm (2") compost.
2 Space the three hyacinth bulbs along the middle of the box.
3 Cover the bulbs with compost until only the tips show.
4 Plant the two arabis plants between the hyacinth bulbs.
5 Firm them in, then top up with compost to within 2.5cm (1") of the rim.
6 Water well. Add more compost if necessary to bring the level back to within 2.5cm (1") of the rim.

Aftercare
Maintain compost moisture throughout the autumn, winter and particularly in the spring, but never water in frosty conditions.

After the bulbs have finished flowering they may be

planted out in the garden. Make sure, however, that they do not dry out until the leaves die down naturally in June or July.

The arabis plants may be used for another display in the autumn and, like the bulbs, can be lifted from the container and planted out in the garden. They prefer partial shade. Cut them back severely after flowering to keep them tidy and encourage them to make new shoots. In the autumn you may wish to lift and divide them ready for use again in containers.

50 MIX AND MATCH

Spring weather does not always allow us as much time outside as we may wish for and you may like to consider your window box as an extension of the room from which you see it. Here we have a framework of pretty curtains complemented by dainty white arabis and bold red tulips.

Site
Window ledge, sun or partial shade.

Container
Large plastic window box 85cm (34") long, 20cm (8") wide, 17.5cm (7") deep.

Planting Time
Early October to mid November.

Looks its Best
The arabis begins to flower in early March and continues for many weeks. The tulips bloom in early April, and are excellent for their sturdiness and length of flowering.

Ingredients
    18 red double early *Tulipa* 'Stockholm'. For an alternative scheme you could buy pink, yellow, orange or carmine varieties
    3 pots or 1 strip of white *Arabis caucasica* 'Snowflake'
    21 litres of compost
    Drainage material such as small pieces of polystyrene

Method
1 Cover the base of the container with 2.5cm (1") drainage material and add 5cm (2") compost.
2 Plant the tulip bulbs in two rows along the length of the box.
3 Cover the bulbs with compost.
4 Whether you are using a strip or pots of arabis, space the plants between the two rows of bulbs so that they will eventually cover the entire box.
5 Make sure all the plants are firmly in place, filling any remaining gaps with compost.
6 Water well. Add more compost if necessary to bring the level to within 2.5cm (1") of the rim.

Aftercare

Keep compost moist throughout the autumn, winter and particularly in the spring, but never water in frosty conditions.

After the bulbs have finished flowering they may be planted out in the garden – make sure, however, that they do not dry out until the leaves die down naturally in June or July.

The arabis should be severely cut back, and then planted out in the garden; it likes well-drained soil in partial shade. You should be able to use it again for a container display in the autumn, by which time you may wish to divide it.

51 DESIGNER BOX

The colours of the curtains are echoed by the soft pink tulips
and the carpet of glorious blue grape hyacinths.

Site
Window ledge, some sun.

Container
Large wooden box, painted white: 80cm (32") long, 20cm
(8") wide, 17.5cm (7") deep.

Planting Time
Early October to mid November.

Looks its Best
Early to late April.

Ingredients
    20 pink double early *Tulipa* 'Peach Blossom'
    30 grape hyacinths *Muscari armeniacum* 'Heavenly Blue'
    20 litres of compost
    Drainage material such as small pieces of polystyrene

Method
1 Cover the base of the container with 2.5cm (1") drainage material and add 5cm (2") compost.
2 Plant the tulip bulbs in two rows along the length of the box.
3 Cover the bulbs with compost until just the tips show.
4 Plant the grape hyacinth bulbs in between the tulips and along the front and back of the box.
5 Cover them with compost.
6 Water well. Add more compost if necessary to bring the level to within 2.5cm (1") of the rim.

Aftercare
Keep the compost moist throughout the autumn, winter and particularly in the spring, but never water in frosty conditions.

After the bulbs have finished flowering, lift the entire contents of the box and carefully plant them out in a sunny part of the garden. Make sure, however, that they do not dry out until the leaves die down naturally in June or July.

The tulips may bloom spasmodically next season but the grape hyacinths will multiply and flower for years.

52 SPRING SALMON

First a winter carpet of pansies, joined in spring by dainty white hyacinths and crowned by rich salmon tulips.

Site
A sunny, sheltered window-sill.

Container
Large Olive Tree terracotta window box: 80cm (32") long, 20cm (8") wide, 17.5cm (7") deep (don't use anything shallower).

Planting Time
September through to November.

Looks its Best
The pansies should flower in all but the worst winter weather, joined by the hyacinths and then by the tulips in early to mid spring.

Ingredients
    12 multiheaded salmon *Tulipa* 'Toronto'
    2 dainty multiheaded Roman hyacinths *Hyacinthus orientalis albulus* 'Snow White'. If unavailable buy the ordinary white bedding type
    4 winter-flowering pansies *Viola* 'Universal White'
    20 litres of compost
    Drainage material such as small pieces of polystyrene

Method
1 Cover the base of the container with 2.5cm (1") of drainage material and add 5cm (2") of compost.
2 Plant eight tulips in a line along the back of the box and four spaced out along the front.
3 Plant the two hyacinths on either side at the front of the box.
4 Cover the bulbs with compost and then plant the four pansies along the centre of the box. Check that they are well balanced.
5 Fill in the remaining gaps with compost. Firm in the pansies.
6 Water well. Add more compost if necessary to bring the level to within 2.5cm (1") of the rim.

Aftercare

Keep the compost moist throughout the autumn, winter and particularly in spring, but never water in frosty conditions. The pansies will soon flag if they become too dry. Deadhead and feed. Feed them regularly throughout the flowering period with a liquid plant feed so that they make a good carpet for the bulbs in spring.

After the hyacinths have finished flowering, carefully remove them from the box and plant them out in the garden where they should continue to flower for years to come. You can try planting out the tulips but they are not so adaptable. Be sure to keep all leaves, stems and roots intact. Make sure they are not allowed to dry out before the leaves die down naturally in June and July. Discard the pansies.

53   A LATE SPRING WINDOW BOX

Easy to plant and to look after, this display will last for a long
time. 'Hawera' is a charming dwarf daffodil, ideal for any
container. Other mid-season choices of daffodil would be
'Thalia' or 'Pancrebar'. Both would look super with the
stunning blue of the grape hyacinths.

Site
Window ledge; any aspect.

Container
Large plastic window box: 85cm (34") long, 20cm (8") wide,
17.5cm (7") deep.

Planting Time
Early September to October.

Looks its Best
Mid to end April.

Ingredients
> 18 multiheaded dwarf daffodils *Narcissus triandrus*
> 'Hawera'
> 36 grape hyacinths *Muscari armeniacum* 'Heavenly Blue'
> 21 litres of compost
> Drainage material such as small pieces of polystyrene

Method
1 Cover the base of the container with 2.5cm (1") drainage
  material and add 5cm (2") compost.
2 Plant daffodil bulbs in two rows at the front and back of
  the box.
3 Cover with compost until just their tips show.
4 Now plant the grape hyacinths in between the daffodil
  bulbs so that their leaves will be less untidy at the front of
  the box.
5 Cover the bulbs with compost, bringing the level to within
  2.5cm (1") of the rim.
6 Water well. Add more compost as necessary to regain its
  former level.

Aftercare
Keep compost moist throughout the autumn, winter

and particularly in the spring, but never water in frosty conditions.

After the bulbs have finished flowering they may be planted out in the garden; make sure, however, they do not dry out until the leaves die down naturally in June or July. Both types of bulbs will do best in a sunny position.

54 SPRING FEVER

Create a lovely hanging basket which will give great pleasure both in autumn and winter and then burst into full colour in early spring.

Site
Hang the basket at eye level. Any aspect but some sun helps.

Container
Wire hanging basket: 35cm (14") in diameter, with a strong 27.5cm (11") bracket.

Planting Time
Early September to early October.

Looks its Best
The primroses will bloom from the time of planting although cold winter weather will halt their flowering until spring. The heathers will be a cascade of white from January onwards, lasting for the entire bulb display which will start in March and continue well into April.

Ingredients
  1 hardy shrub *Euonymus japonicus* 'Aureopictus'
  2 heathers *Erica herbacea* 'Springwood White'
  1 variegated ivy *Hedera helix* 'Glacier'
  2 primroses, *Primula vulgaris*, one yellow and one brick-orange. Any from the 'Husky' range would be excellent
  6 dwarf *Tulipa kaufmanniana* 'Shakespeare'
  10 daffodils *Narcissus cyclamineus* 'Tête à Tête'
  10 mixed *Crocus aureus* 'Dutch Yellow' and '*Crocus vernus*' 'Purpureus Grandiflorus'
  10 litres of compost
  Moss; *see* page 21
  Circle of plastic the size of a dinner plate

Method (All top planted)
  1 Line the basket with a generous thickness of moss, starting at the base and bringing it well up the sides so that you form a collar above the rim of the basket.
  2 Cut four 2.5cm (1") slits in the plastic circle and place over the moss lining in the bottom of the basket. Cover with 2.5cm (1") compost.

3 Place the euonymus at the back of the basket.
4 Place the heathers on either side of the euonymus so that they spread over the rim.
5 Place the ivy so that it trails down the front.
6 Plant the primroses to the right and left of the ivy so that they add winter colour to the front of the basket.
7 Plant the tulip bulbs between the euonymus and the heathers at the back of the basket.
8 Plant the daffodil bulbs in the centre of the basket.
9 Cover with compost until just the tips show.
10 Plant the crocus corms in any remaining gaps.
11 Make sure that the plants and bulbs are firmly in place.
12 Water well. Add more compost to bring the level to within 2.5cm (1") of the rim.

Aftercare
Keep compost moist throughout the autumn, winter and particularly in the spring, but never water in frosty conditions. Protect in severe weather. Feed the basket in early March and early April.

After the bulbs have finished flowering they may be planted out in the garden. However, make sure that they do not dry out until the leaves die down naturally in June or July. The rest of the plants may be used for another display in the autumn and, like the bulbs, they can be planted out in the garden.

55   A BASKET FULL OF CHEER

Yellow violas and pink daisies provide welcome colour in all but the depths of winter, and are joined in spring by these pretty pink tulips.

Yellow violas and pink daisies provide much welcome colour.

Site
Sheltered and sunny.

Container
Wire hanging basket: 35cm (14") in diameter with a sturdy 27.5cm (11") bracket.

Planting Time
September to October – the earlier the better, then the bedding plants can get well established before the winter.

Looks its best
It should flower in all but the depths of winter and be at its best in mid spring.

Ingredients
   2 strips of yellow violas *Viola* 'Prince John'
   6 pink early dwarf *Tulipa* 'Peach Blossom'
   2 strips of pink daisies *Bellis perennis* 'Tasso Rose'
  10 litres of compost
   Moss; *see* page 21
   Circle of plastic about the size of a saucer

Method
1 Line the basket with a generous thickness of moss, start at the base and bring it a third of the way up the sides.
2 Cut five 2.5cm (1") slits in the plastic lining and put it in place at the bottom of the basket.
3 Cover the base of the lining with 5cm (2") of compost.
4 Carefully divide up the strips of plants.
5 Using the violas, plant eight of them evenly around the base of the basket by passing the roots through a hole you have made in the moss. Be sure they make good contact with the compost.
6 Close any gaps with moss, and bring the level up around the sides by another 5cm (2").

7 Plant the tulip bulbs in the middle of the basket and add another 5cm (2") of compost.
8 Now use eight daisies to make another ring of plants, using the same method as described above.
9 Again plug any gaps in the moss and bring the level to the rim of the basket. Add more compost.
10 Now, using a mixture of violas and daisies, plant another eight alternately through the moss in a ring underneath the rim.
11 Add any final bits of moss to make sure there are no remaining gaps in the wall of moss.
12 Plant the remaining violas and daisies around the edge of the top of the basket.
13 Water well. Add more compost and moss if necessary.

Aftercare
Keep compost moist throughout the autumn, winter and particularly in spring, but never water in frosty weather. Protect in severe weather. Feed the basket regularly throughout the flowering period so that it makes a good carpet for the bulbs in early spring. Deadhead the violas and daisies. After flowering is complete, discard all the plants.

AUTUMN, WINTER AND SPRING WICKER BASKETS

56 AN EARLY SPRING BASKET

What an unusual present. All you need is a deep basket with a high handle and a generous planting of bulbs.

Site
Preferably some sun to open up the crocus flowers.

Container
A wicker or bamboo basket: about 50cm (20") long, 15cm (6") deep, 40cm (16") wide. Give it three coats of yacht varnish to preserve it outdoors.

Planting Time
Early September to mid October.

Looks its Best
March to early April.

Ingredients
    20 daffodils *Narcissus cyclamineus* 'February Gold'
    30 purple *Crocus vernus* 'Purpureus Grandiflorus'
    Moss (only if you have an open bamboo basket)
    25 litres of compost
    4 handfuls of horticultural grit as drainage material
    Black plastic sheeting cut to fit inside the basket

Method
1 If you have an open bamboo basket, line it with a generous thickness of moss. Start at the base and bring it well up the sides to form a collar above the rim of the basket.
2 Whatever sort of basket you are using, cut six 2.5cm (1") slits in the plastic sheeting and line the base and sides with it.
3 Cover the lining with the grit and add 5cm (2") compost.
4 Plant the daffodil bulbs evenly over the central area, then cover with compost until just the tips show.

5 Plant the crocus corms around and between the daffodil bulbs. Firm them into the compost, water lightly and then top up with more compost to bring the level to within 2.5cm (1") of the rim.

6 Any odd pieces of plastic lining which still show should now be trimmed off or tucked under the compost.

7 Find a sheltered home for the basket during the winter, raised off the ground and near the wall of the house. It needs moisture so don't cover it.

8 When it comes into flower, bring it to a sunny position near a window so that it can be enjoyed to the full.

Aftercare

Keep the compost moist throughout the autumn, winter and particularly in the spring, but never water in frosty conditions.

After the bulbs have finished flowering, lift them carefully out of the basket and plant direct in the garden. Make sure that they do not dry out until the leaves die down naturally in June or July.

57 THE WISHING-WELL BASKET

Inspired by the story of the little girl picking flowers for her grandmother, this basket contains a tulip called 'Red Riding Hood' and a mass of white anemones.

Site
The sunnier the better.

Container
Wicker basket: 32.5cm (13") in diameter, 15cm (6") deep. Apply three coats of yacht varnish to preserve it outdoors.

Planting Time
September to late October.

Looks its Best
Late February to mid April.

Ingredients
- 20 *Tulipa gregii* 'Red Riding Hood', a bright red tulip with striking purple veins in its leaves
- 30 *Anemone blanda* 'White Splendour'
- 10 litres of compost
- 4 handfuls of horticultural grit as drainage material
- Black plastic lining cut to fit the bottom and sides of the basket

Method
1 Line the basket with the black plastic and make six 2.5cm (1") slits along the bottom to provide drainage holes.
2 Cover the lining with grit and add 5cm (2") of compost.
3 Gently firm the tulip bulbs into the compost, trying to avoid contact with each other or the sides of the basket.
4 Cover the bulbs with compost until just the tips show.
5 Plant the anemones between the tulips but concentrate them mainly around the outer edge.
6 Add more compost and bring the level to within 2.5cm (1") of the rim.
7 Water lightly and add more compost if necessary.
8 Any odd bits of plastic lining still showing should be trimmed off or tucked under the compost. Find a sheltered spot for it to sit during the winter e.g. near the wall of the house; it needs moisture so don't cover it up but do raise

it off the ground slightly so that the bottom can remain dry. Protect it further in very severe weather.

9 In early March bring the basket into a sunny spot where you can enjoy it to the full.

Aftercare

Keep compost moist throughout the autumn, winter and particularly in spring, but never water in frosty conditions. After flowering the bulbs may be planted out in the garden. The tulips may not do well but the anemones should flower for years. The basket can now be used again for a summer planting but give it another coat of yacht varnish first.

58   A BASKET OF DAINTY
DAFFODILS

Creamy daffodils and pretty blue and white grape hyacinths make a charming basket together. It would make a wonderful Easter present.

Site
Any.

Container
Wicker basket: 37.5cm (15") long, 25cm (10") wide, 15cm (6") deep. Before use, apply three coats of yacht varnish to preserve it outdoors.

Planting Time
September to October.

Looks its Best
From early to mid spring, a long-lasting display.

Ingredients
- 25 *Narcissus tazetta* 'Minnow'; multiheaded cream and yellow daffodils
- 20 white grape hyacinths *Muscari botryoides* 'Album'
- 10 grape hyacinths *Muscari armeniacum* 'Heavenly Blue'
- 12 litres of compost
- 4 handfuls of horticultural grit as drainage material
- Black plastic lining cut to fit the bottom and sides of the basket

Method
1 Line the basket with the black plastic and make six 2.5cm (1") slits in the centre to provide drainage holes.
2 Cover the lining with grit and add 5cm (2") of compost.
3 Gently firm the daffodil bulbs into the compost, trying to avoid contact with each other or the sides of the basket.
4 Cover the bulbs with compost so that just the tips show.
5 Plant the grape hyacinths between the daffodils, mixing the two colours as you do so.
6 Add more compost and bring the level to within 2.5cm (1") of the rim.
7 Water lightly and add more compost if necessary.

8 Any plastic lining still showing should be trimmed off.
9 Find a sheltered, sunny spot for this basket during the winter e.g. near the wall of the house but don't cover it up as it needs moisture. Raise it off the ground slightly so that water is not trapped underneath. Protect it in very severe weather by bringing it into a cold garage or barn.
10 In early March put the basket into its final flowering position, somewhere sunny and near to the house where you can enjoy it for many weeks.

Aftercare
Keep compost moist throughout the autumn, winter and early spring, but never water in frosty conditions. After flowering, all the bulbs may be planted in the garden where they will flower for many years.

59 A BASKET OF LATE SPRING FLOWERS

Another idea for a basket, this time filled with late spring flowers – dainty dwarf daffodils and simple but ever-popular forget-me-nots.

Site
Partial shade.

Container
Wicker basket: 35cm (14") long, 22.5cm (9") wide, 20cm (8") deep. Preserve it with three coats of yacht varnish for outdoors.

Planting Time
Early September to early October.

Looks its Best
Mid to late April.

Ingredients
- 30 dwarf yellow daffodils *Narcissus triandrus* 'Hawera'. (The display would still be lovely with only 20 bulbs.)
- 2 strips pink and blue forget-me-nots *Myosotis alpestris*. If you can't buy pink don't worry – the basket will still be pretty with just blue
- 14 litres of compost
- 2 handfuls of horticultural grit as drainage material
- Black plastic lining cut to fit inside the basket

Method
1 Cut some black plastic to line the basket and make six 2.5cm (1") slits along the bottom to provide drainage holes.
2 Cover the liner with grit and add 5cm (2") compost.
3 Gently firm the daffodil bulbs into the compost, trying to avoid contact with each other or with the sides of the basket.
4 Cover the bulbs with compost to bring the level to within 2.5cm (1") of the rim.
5 Carefully separate the forget-me-nots. Plant five of each colour alternately around the edge of the basket.
6 Make sure all the plants are firmly in place.

7 Water well. Add more compost if necessary to bring the level to within 2.5cm (1") of the rim.

8 Any odd pieces of plastic lining still showing should now be trimmed off or tucked into the compost.

9 Find a sunny sheltered outdoor home for the basket during the winter, e.g. raised off the ground near the wall of the house. It needs moisture so don't cover it.

10 Then in spring, bring it within view of a window where it can be fully appreciated.

Aftercare

Forget-me-nots like moisture so take care to check that the compost is moist throughout the autumn, winter and particularly in the spring, but never water in frosty conditions. After the bulbs have finished flowering they may be planted out in the garden. Make sure, however, that they do not dry out until the leaves die down naturally in June or July. The forget-me-nots can be allowed to self-seed; in which case, plant them out in the garden.

AUTUMN, WINTER AND SPRING URNS AND POTS

60 FIRE IN A CHIMNEY POT

Here is a very tall chimney pot sitting in a London basement. The pansies were in flower throughout the autumn and winter, except in all but the worst weather. In spring, they were joined by fiery red tulips.

Site
Any aspect, although prefers some sun.

Container
Small plastic or terracotta container to fit inside the top of the chimney pot. The one shown is 25cm (10") in diameter.

Planting Time
Early October to mid November

Looks its Best
The yellow pansies should flower throughout the winter, except in the coldest spells. The tulips will bloom in early April.

Ingredients
  1 variegated ivy *Hedera helix* 'Harald'
  20 multiheaded red *Tulipa praestans* 'Tubergen's Variety'
  2 winter-flowering pansies *Viola* 'Universal Yellow with Blotch'
  8 litres of compost
  Drainage material such as small pieces of polystyrene

Method
  1 Cover the base of the inner container with 2.5cm (1") drainage material and add 5cm (2") compost.
  2 Position the ivy at the front of the container.
  3 Plant ten tulip bulbs at the base of the container, behind the ivy.
  4 Cover with compost until just their tips show.
  5 Now make a double layer with the other ten bulbs, plant-

ing them in between the bulb tips of the bottom layer.

6 Add more compost so that the bulbs are completely covered.

7 Plant the two pansies on either side of the ivy. Here they appear only on one side because they have both been drawn towards the sun.

8 Make sure that all the plants are firmly in place, filling any remaining gaps with compost.

9 Water well. Add more compost if necessary to bring the level to within 2.5cm (1") of the rim.

10 Lift the container and place it carefully in the chimney pot.

Aftercare

Keep compost moist throughout the autumn, winter and particularly in the spring, but never water in frosty conditions. Pansies are thirsty drinkers and will soon flag if lacking. The pansies should be deadheaded regularly and be given a liquid feed from early spring onwards.

Discard the bulbs and pansies after flowering, but replant the ivy ready for another display in the summer.

61 THE DAISY POT

'Robella' is a charming new daisy with stunning large pink flowers; a perfect partner for the beautiful 'Anne Marie' hyacinths and soft blue primroses.

Site
Sun or partial shade, sheltered.

Container
Kingfisher stone pot 42.5cm (17") diameter, 30cm (12") deep.

Planting Time
September to October.

Looks its Best
March to April.

Ingredients
>   1 *Polyanthus* 'Crescendo Blue'
>   4 pink *Hyacinthus orientalis* 'Anne Marie'
>   2 variegated ivies *Hedera helix* 'Kolibri'
>   4 blue primroses *Primula vulgaris* from the 'Husky' series
>   4 pink daisies *Bellis perennis* 'Robella'
>   10 *Anemone blanda* 'White Splendour'
>   32 litres of compost
>   Drainage material such as small pieces of polystyrene

Method
1 Cover the base of the pot with 5cm (2") drainage material and bring the compost level to within 2.5cm (1") of the rim.
2 Plant the polyanthus in the centre surrounded by a circle of hyacinths. Bury the bulbs so that they are covered by twice their depth in compost.
3 Plant the ivies on either side of the pot.
4 Alternate the blue primroses and pink daisies around the edge.
5 Plant the anemones 5cm (2") deep in any of the gaps.
6 Water well. Add more compost if necessary.

Aftercare
Place the pot in a sheltered spot. In severe weather, protect

it in a garage or put it beside the house wall surrounded by sacking. Keep the compost moist throughout the season, but never water in frosty conditions. Feed every fortnight from early March until daisies have finished flowering. In late May transfer the plants and bulbs to the garden.

62 THE WARWICK VASE

This planting scheme is based on a suggestion made by H. T. Martin of Stoneleigh in *The Gardener* magazine in November 1900.

Site
Sun or partial shade.

Container
This lead container is styled after the famous Warwick vase and is made by Renaissance Casting. The diameter is 35cm (14") and the inside planting depth is 22.5cm (9").

Planting Time
September to October.

Looks its Best
The bulbs will bloom from early March through to April. However, the golden colourings of the thymes and euonymus ensure that the container is delightful throughout the entire season.

Ingredients
    1 *Euonymus fortunei* 'Emerald 'n' Gold'; low growing with gold, pink and green leaves
    5 white *Hyacinthus orientalis* 'L'Innocence'
    1 *Arabis caucasica* (syn. *A. albida*) 'Variegata'
    3 golden thyme *Thymus* × *citriodorus* 'Aureus'
    15 yellow and white *Crocus aureus* 'Dutch Yellow' and *Crocus vernus* 'Jeanne d'Arc' mixed
    14 litres of compost
    Drainage material such as small pieces of polystyrene

Method
1 Cover the base of the container with 5cm (2") of drainage material and add 5cm (2") of compost.
2 Plant the euonymus towards the centre-back of the base and place the five hyacinth bulbs around it. Cover the bulbs with compost.
3 Plant the arabis close to the rim at the centre-front of the pot with a thyme on either side. Plant the third thyme behind the euonymus.
4 Fill in the gaps with more compost so that the level is

brought to within 2.5cm (1") of the rim of the container.
5 Space the crocus corms in between the plants. Push them well down so that they are covered by at least 2.5cm (1") of compost.
6 Water well. Make sure all the plants are firmly in place and that the arrangement looks well balanced. Add more compost if necessary.

Aftercare
Keep compost moist throughout the autumn, winter and spring but never water in frosty conditions. After the crocuses have finished flowering, carefully remove them from the container as the leaves will grow very long and spoil the arrangement when the hyacinths are in bloom. They should come out quite easily and can be planted elsewhere in the garden. Once the hyacinths have finished flowering they, and all the other plants, can be transferred to the garden. Cut the arabis back hard after it has flowered to encourage neat growth for the following year.

63   THE TRIUMPHANT ATILLA

The pale primrose wallflowers, and violet tulips make an appealing colour scheme. A gentle fragrance comes from the wallflowers, filling the late spring air.

Site
Prefers a sunny spot, sheltered from strong winds.

Container
A wooden tub or half-barrel: 60cm (24") in diameter, 42.5cm (17") deep.

Planting Time
Early October.

Looks its Best
From mid April to end May.

Ingredients
8 dwarf wallflowers *Cheiranthus* 'Primrose Bedder'. Buy a bunch of ten and choose the best eight. Look for strong sturdy plants that have branched out well – not tall, limp, straggly ones. As soon as you have purchased them, open up the bunch and give them a good drink before planting
10 late medium tall *Tulipa* 'Atilla' of the Triumph type
100 litres of compost
Plenty of crocks or pieces of polystyrene as drainage material

Method
1 Cover the base of the container with 5cm (2") drainage material and cover with 20cm (8") compost.
2 Plant six of the tulip bulbs in a wide circle with four in the centre.
3 Cover the bulbs with compost until just the tips show.
4 Choose eight of the best developed wallflowers, make a circle of five of them near the outer edge and three in the centre but avoid placing directly over the tulips. Add compost around each one until the base of the stem is covered. If you have a garden you may like to plant out the remaining plants, then if you lose any of the ones in the pot (and you may), you will have a replacement.

5 Water well. Firm down the plants and top up with compost where necessary, leaving at least a 2.5cm (1") gap
between the compost and the rim of the barrel.

Aftercare
Keep compost moist throughout the autumn, winter and
spring but never water in frosty weather. Wind seems to do
more damage than heavy snow or frost, so try to place the
pot in a sheltered area. Apply a liquid feed in early and late
April.

When the wallflowers have finished flowering discard
them. Lift the tulips with as many of the roots intact as
possible and replant them in a sunny spot in the garden.

64   A PERSIAN CARPET IN A BARREL

Rich yellows and oranges radiate from this simple planting of tulips and wallflowers. It makes a warm welcome to any front door where it can be enjoyed not only for its colours but also for its delicious scent.

Site
Sunny.

Container
Wooden half-barrel or large pot: 60cm (24") in diameter, 40cm (16") deep. A plastic tub sits inside the barrel so that the wood does not come into contact with the compost.

Planting Time
Early October.

Looks its Best
Mid to late spring.

Ingredients
   12 mid-season Darwin hybrid tulips *Tulipa* 'Beauty of Apeldoorn'
   8 wallflower plants *Cheiranthus cheiri* 'Persian Carpet'. *See* page 144
   92 litres of compost
   Plenty of crocks or pieces of polystyrene as drainage material

Method
1 Cover the base of the container with 5cm (2") of drainage material and add 20cm (8") of compost.
2 Plant the tulips in two wide circles, eight in the outer one and four in the inner one. Mark their shape with sticks.
3 Add more compost to bring the level to within 5cm (2") of the rim.
4 Plant five wallflower plants in between the two circles of tulips, saving the last three for the centre. By planting the wallflowers close together they seem better protected during the winter.
5 Water well. Firm down the plants and top up with more compost where necessary, leaving at least a 2.5cm (1") gap between the compost and the rim of the container.

Aftercare

Keep compost moist throughout the autumn, winter and spring, but never water in frosty weather. Wind seems to damage wallflowers more than heavy frost or snow, so keep the barrel in a sheltered area. Don't despair if you wake up to see the leaves all floppy after a bad frost the night before. By midday they will probably look as perky as they normally do. They can withstand quite low temperatures. Apply a liquid feed in early and late April.

Discard the wallflowers after flowering. Remove the tulips, keeping the roots intact as much as possible, and plant them in the garden. They should flower well another year. Make sure they do not dry out until their leaves die down naturally in June or July.

65   WALLFLOWERS AND BELLIS DAISIES IN A POT

Pale yellow wallflowers and pretty pink bellis daisies form a scented pyramid which will last for many weeks.

Site
Sunny aspect, sheltered from strong winds.

Container
Medium sized terracotta pot; 35cm (14") in diameter, 30cm (12") deep.

Planting Time
Early October. In some areas you may have to wait until early spring for the bellis daisies.

Looks its Best
From early spring until the end of May.

Ingredients
- 1 bunch of dwarf wallflowers *Cheiranthus* 'Primrose Bedder'; *see* page 144
- 1 strip of pink daisies *Bellis perennis* 'Tasso Rose' or 'Robella'
- 22 litres of compost
- Drainage material such as small pieces of polystyrene

Method
1 Cover the base of the container with 5cm (2") drainage material and add about 15cm (6") compost.
2 Choose seven of the best developed wallflower plants and make a circle of five of them near the outer edge. Add compost around each one until the base of the stem is covered. Then plant the remaining two in the central area, again mounding up the soil around the roots until the base of the stem is covered. If you have a garden, you may like to plant out the smaller plants; then if you lose any of the ones in the pot you will have a replacement.
3 If you are able to buy bellis in the autumn, carefully separate the plants in the strip and insert around the edge of the pot. You might have to wait until early spring, when you will find them more readily available.

4 Water well, firming down the plants, and topping up with compost where necessary. Leave at least 2.5cm (1") between the compost and the rim of the pot.

Aftercare
Keep the compost moist throughout the autumn, winter and spring but never water in frosty conditions. Wind seems to do more damage to the wallflowers than heavy snow or frost, so try to place the pot in a sheltered area. Apply a liquid feed in early and late April.

When the wallflowers have finished flowering, empty the pot and discard all the contents although the bellis could be enjoyed for several more weeks in the garden if preferred.

66 SCARLET TULIPS AND PRIMULAS

Some of these primulas are a perfect match for the scarlet tulips and provide a dazzling carpet to show off the rich tones of the upper blooms with their dark black centres.

Site
Sunny.

Container
Erin planter: 40cm (16") in diameter, 32.5cm (13") deep. Any medium to large pot would be appropriate.

Planting Time
Late September to November.

Looks its Best
Mid to late spring.

Ingredients
- 8 *Tulipa* 'Olaf' with scarlet flowers and contrasting black centres
- 5 *Polyanthus* 'Crescendo Mixed'
- 31 litres of compost
- Drainage material such as small pieces of polystyrene

Method
1 Cover the base of the container with 5cm (2") of drainage material and then add 12.5cm (5") of compost.
2 Plant the tulip bulbs well spaced out so that they are right away from the sides of the container and are not touching each other.
3 Add more compost to bring the level to within 5cm (2") of the rim and plant the polyanthus around the edge of the container.
4 Water well. Firm in the plants and add more compost if necessary to bring the level to within 2.5cm (1") of the rim.

Aftercare
Keep compost moist throughout the autumn, winter and early spring. Apply a liquid feed in early spring once the polyanthus begin to flower and need the extra boost.

   After the bulbs have finished flowering, empty the contents of the pot. Plant the polyanthus in a moist part of the garden where they will grow and multiply ready for division and use in the autumn. The tulips may not fare well another year but if you have light soil and want to try them in a sunny spot, plant out with minimum disturbance to their roots. Do not allow them to dry out until the leaves have died down naturally in the early summer.

67   THE LOVELY ANGELIQUE

'Angelique' has the softest pink flowers which look very pretty rising out of a bed of blue anemones.

Site
Sheltered and sunny.

Container
Large handthrown terracotta pot (made by Whichford Pottery): 47.5cm (19") in diameter, 32.5cm (13") deep.

Planting Time
Late September to November.

Look its Best
The anemones will be in flower from early spring onwards joined by the tulips in mid to late spring.

Ingredients
      20 *Tulipa* 'Angelique'; tall double pink
      20 blue *Anemone blanda*. Forget-me-nots would give a
          similar carpet effect
      44 litres of compost
      Drainage material such as small pieces of polystyrene

Method
1 Cover the base of the container with 5cm (2") of drainage material and add 12cm (5") of compost.
2 Plant the tulip bulbs well spaced out, right away from the sides of the container and without touching each other.
3 Add more compost to bring the level to within 2.5cm (1") of the rim.
4 Plant the anemones about 5cm (2") deep, all around the pot but concentrated mainly near the edge.
5 Water well.

Aftercare
Keep compost moist throughout the autumn, winter and spring, but never water in frosty weather. Protect in windy and very wet weather when the tulips are in flower. They have large heads and can be damaged more easily than single tulips. Placed in a sheltered spot, however, this should not be a problem.

After flowering, plant the anemones in the garden where they will multiply. The tulips may not do so well another year but you may like to try them in light soil in a sunny spot.

Try not to disturb the roots too much when you replant and keep them watered until the leaves die down naturally in the early summer.

68   A WEDDING DAY POT

This charming combination makes a perfect display to grace any spring wedding, although you don't have to have that excuse to plant it!

Site
Some sun preferred.

Container
Large terracotta pot: 37.5cm (15") in diameter, 37.5cm (15") deep.

Planting Time
Early October to early November.

Looks its Best
This kind of arabis will flower in early April followed by the bulbs in the middle of the month.

Ingredients
- 8 pink daffodils *Narcissus* 'Salome'; the trumpets will begin as yellow and then change to apricot pink as they mature
- 7 mid season *Tulipa* 'White Virgin'
- 3 double white *Arabis caucasica* 'Flore Pleno'
- 36 litres of compost
- Drainage material such as small pieces of polystyrene

Method
1 Cover the base of the container with 2.5cm (1") drainage material and add 15cm (6") compost.
2 Arrange five daffodil bulbs in a circle about 10cm (4") from the edge of the pot, with three more in the middle.
3 Cover the bulbs with the compost until just the tips show, then plant the tulip bulbs in a slightly smaller circle than the daffodils.
4 Bring the compost level to within 2.5cm (1") of the rim.
5 Plant the arabis around the edge of the container, making sure that they are firmly in place.
6 Water well. Add more compost if necessary to bring the level to within 2.5cm (1") of the rim.

Aftercare
Keep compost moist throughout the autumn, winter and particularly in the spring, but never water in frosty conditions. After the bulbs have finished flowering they may be planted out in the garden. Make sure, however, that they do not dry out until the leaves die down naturally in June or July. Tulips prefer a sunny home but be warned – these might not perform well in future seasons.

Remove the arabis and plant in partial shade. Early summer is the ideal time to cut it back to encourage a good shape for next season. In the autumn it can be lifted and divided for use again in containers.

69   APRICOT BEAUTY

'Apricot Beauty' is one of my favourite tulips. As the flower
matures the colour changes subtly to a deeper shade of apricot and as the bloom opens in the sunlight all sorts of delicate salmons, pinks and apricots are revealed inside. It is
wonderful as a cut flower ... if you can spare the odd one
from the pot!

Site
Sunny.

Container
Large terracotta pot: 30cm (12") in diameter, 27.5cm (11")
deep.

Planting Time
Late September to November.

Looks its Best
The pansies should flower throughout the winter in all but
the worst weather, and are joined by the tulips in early to
mid spring. This would make a lovely display for a mid
spring wedding.

Ingredients
    12 *Tulipa* 'Apricot Beauty'
    3 white winter-flowering pansies *Viola* 'Universal White'.
       Alternatively, use cream-coloured pansies but no strong
       colours
    12 litres of compost
    Drainage material such as small pieces of polystyrene

Method
1 Cover the base of the container with 7.5cm (3") of drainage
   material and add 5cm (2") of compost.
2 Plant the tulip bulbs firmly in the compost so that they
   form a balanced group. Space them out well so that they
   are not touching each other or the sides of the container.
3 Cover with more compost to bring the level to within 5cm
   (2") of the rim.
4 Plant the three pansies around the edge of the pot.
5 Water well. Firm in the plants and add more compost if
   necessary.

Aftercare

Keep compost moist throughout the autumn, winter and spring. The pansies will soon flag when they are thirsty, but never water in frosty weather. Apply a liquid feed in late March, and deadhead to prolong flowering. Discard contents in May.

70   THE ORANGE EMPEROR

This is a simple but effective planting scheme which combines the rich orange of the tulip with the brilliant blue of the grape hyacinth. It looks especially beautiful in the terracotta pot but would be suitable for any wooden or stone container.

Site
Sun or partial shade.

Container
Terracotta pot: 30cm (12") in diameter, 25 (10") deep.

Planting Time
October to November.

Looks its Best
Mid spring.

Ingredients
> 12 *Tulipa fosteriana* 'Orange Emperor'; a rich orange tulip with a large flower and sturdy, short stem. Alternatively, use 'Red', 'White' or 'Yellow Emperor'
> 20 grape hyacinths *Muscari armeniacum* 'Heavenly Blue'
> 12 litres of compost
> Drainage material such as small pieces of polystyrene

Method
1 Cover the base of the container with 5cm (2") of drainage material and add 5cm (2") of compost.
2 Space the tulip bulbs in the middle of the container. Take care that they do not touch each other or the sides of the pot.
3 Cover with compost so that just their tips show.
4 Plant the grape hyacinths in between the tulips but concentrate most around the edge of the container.
5 Cover with compost and bring the level up to within 2.5cm (1") of the rim.
6 Water well and add more compost if necessary.

Aftercare
Keep the compost moist throughout the autumn, winter and spring, but never water in frosty weather.

After flowering, plant the contents in a sunny part of the garden. Be careful not to disturb the roots. The grape hyacinths will cheerfully reappear year after year. The tulips may not perform so well.

INDEX